CRACKS

Memoir of a Southern Plowboy

By

John Buck Miller

Copyright © 2024 by John Miller

All rights reserved.

ISBN- 979-8-218-59724-5

Formatting/Text design by Watercress Press, San Antonio, Texas.

Cover design by Hammad of Hmd Publishing

No portion of this book may be reproduced in any form without written permission from the publisher or author, except as permitted by U.S. copyright law.

Dedication

I dedicate this memoir to those who call me Dad and Papaw. Leticia, Michelle, Layne, Neal, Grace, and Hope, you are the brightest threads in the tapestry of my life and the most precious gifts God has given me.

Acknowledgements

They say everyone has one book in them. *Cracks* is mine. Two very special women made this man's dream a reality. One has been my constant companion for over six decades; the other came into my life just over a year ago and has played a major role in compiling my stories, letters, and notes into book format.

First and foremost, I want to express my utmost gratitude, appreciation, and admiration to my beautiful wife, Emma, who has been my steadfast source of strength and support for the last sixty-four years. She came into my life when I was still reeling from an upbringing riddled with family dysfunction, poverty, and limited resources. Emma saw in me the man she and God have helped me become. Side-by-side and hand-in-hand, we have traveled this road of life navigating some seemingly endless stretches of rough terrain as well as distances filled with adventure, joy, and excitement. We have shared countless moments filled with joy and heartbreak, laughter and tears, successes and failures. Regardless of life's circumstances, my beautiful wife's love and support have never faltered. God sure smiled on ol' John Buck when he sent her to me. Thank you, Emma, for being my everything.

I also wish to express my appreciation to Toni McMahan, the daughter of one of my oldest and dearest friends, Tommy Hodges. Tommy and I met at Henderson State College when we were both, after serving in the military, struggling to simultaneously pursue higher education and start our families. I lost touch with my old friend for a number of years before sending him a letter just over a year ago hoping to rekindle our neglected friendship. His daughter, Toni, responded on his behalf and became my pen pal. I enjoyed her letters and her unique writing style, so I eventually asked her if she might be willing to help me fulfil my dream of compiling my life's experiences into a book for my children, grandchildren, family, and friends—known and unknown—to enjoy. She agreed and her assistance in organizing my manuscript has been invaluable. I will forever be thankful to her for the gifts of her time and talents as we have worked together to bring *Cracks* from a collection of random stories, documents, and letters into a coherent collection of cherished memories. Thank you, Cupcake!

Contents

Eyes 1

Meet the Family 26

Let's Talk Military 38

Near-death Experience at Francois Creek 68

Grandpaw's Brother Becomes Murder Suspect 90

Roadside Ruckuses..99

The Hunting Cap Tunnel................................110

Gambling Man...114

Tom and Jerry 125

The Last Chapter 129

Eyes

No one could spin a story quite like my fraternal grandfather, Roy Miller, who was one of the most colorful individuals I've ever known. He was of German descent. My ancestors, most of whom had red or sandy-colored hair, left Germany as Meullers in 1904, changing the surname to Miller in America. They originally settled in Kansas and Nebraska before coming to Arkansas in 1916. Some of the Millers of this lineage still call central Arkansas their home.

Grandpaw Miller was a cheerful soul who was well-liked and respected by all who knew him. Grandmaw (Maud) Miller, on the other hand, was a mean-spirited and grouchy woman. I suppose their union is proof that opposites attract.

Grandpaw was a major influence in my life. He liked pretty women and never failed to admire his five daughters-in-law; yet, he always conducted himself as a gentleman. Storytelling was one of Grandpaw Miller's many God-given talents. I loved listening to his tales, and he loved telling them, so we made a pretty good pair. His stories that I grew up hearing over and over are the primary sources of information regarding my birth and early years of life.

Grandpaw and Grandmaw lived about two miles, as the crow flies, from our home and were our closest neighbors. According to Grandpaw, an inordinate amount of rainfall made the early fall of 1935 an unusually unpleasant one for residents of central Arkansas. On the date of my birth, September 22, floodwaters from nearby creeks and the Saline River covered the dirt road that led to our house and prevented the country doctor from making the journey to our home for my delivery. In those days, only the wealthy or those mothers with serious pregnancy complications went to a hospital to give birth. Back then, giving birth was treated as a sickness and new mothers remained bedfast for a few days after having a baby. Most babies in rural Arkansas were born in their family homes with neighbor women assisting with the delivery and then caring for the mother and baby a few days afterwards. My poor mother went into labor two months early with only my father to help with my delivery. At birth, I weighed slightly less than three pounds. What a whopper! I spent my first winter in a shoe box. Nobody expected me to survive.

My father used to tell of his morning routine during my infancy which was to roll out of bed at 4:30 a.m. and start a fire in the old pot-bellied wood stove. That stove was our only source of heat in our drafty old shanty. My father's rustling about would awaken me, and I would begin to squirm and fuss. He would peek into the shoe box.

Seeing my movements and hearing my whimpering, he would shout back to my mom, "Chloe, he's still alive!"

Each time my father told this story, I got the distinct impression that both he and my mother would have been greatly relieved if there had been no sound or movement coming from my shoebox crib.

My mother gave birth to three children in as many years. When I made my debut onto the world stage, my sister, Mary Lou, was three years old and my brother, Charles, was sixteen months. Because Mother had nursed three babies with no reprieve in between, her breast milk dried up. What little milk I could get was not sufficient to sustain me. My chances of living to see another sunrise diminished with each passing day.

It just so happened that Grandpaw owned a nanny goat that had just given birth and had a plentiful supply of milk. Grandpaw led that old nanny and her newborn kid two miles through those rugged woods to our house. For the next two years that old nanny produced plenty of good, rich goat milk—enough to provide all the necessary nutrients for both her kid and me to grow and flourish.

Two weeks after my birth, my father borrowed a car from his dad to make the eleven-mile trip to

Malvern, Arkansas, to inform the doctor of my birth. This set the wheels in motion to legally record my birth. The doctor eventually made a home visit to verify my existence and complete my birth certificate. Upon arriving at our home, his top priority seemed to be to finish his job as quickly as possible and then get the heck out of Dodge. It was as though he thought our impoverished condition might be contagious.

In his haste, he made a mess of the legal document that would follow me for the rest of my life. On the birth certificate, he indicated that my birth was in Fenter Township in Hot Spring County when it was actually in Fenter, Arkansas, in Grant County. He also misspelled my name, recording Johnnie instead of Johnny. The name on my birth certificate was of little consequence for the first eighteen years of my life and served merely as a jumping off point for a fitting nickname.

Few Southern kids were called by a single name. Double-word names such as Billy Bob, Sally Ann, Mable Lou, and Herman Lee were common. John Buck is the double-word name that was dubbed for me and that has stayed with me throughout my life. Other nicknames given to me for periods of time along my journey have included John Franklin, Runt, Johnny Reb, Arkansas Ridgerunner, and Janitor—each with a story attached. None have endured the test of time like ol' John Buck. Although the mistakes on my birth certificate initially posed no problems, that snooty backwoods physician's errors eventually caught up with and plagued me throughout my early adult life.

My immediate family—consisting of my parents, two older siblings, and a younger brother—lived in a two-room log shanty that had a pine-shingle roof. Both rooms of our cabin were small and crowded. Our humble abode was in an area of central Arkansas where the corners of Grant, Hot Spring, and Saline counties converged.

We had no electricity, indoor plumbing, or running water (except the running water that ran from a nearby spring a quarter mile from our home). The kitchen housed a wood cook stove and a small kitchen table with three chairs and a bench. A cast-iron skillet that was used for most of the cooking occupied a permanent position on the stove's surface along with two flat irons that Mother used to press the wrinkles out of our clothes. The rest of our cookware hung from the walls in the kitchen.

There were two "eyes" on top of the stove. These were cast-iron discs that sat in the holes on the top of the stove. They were normally left in place when cooking to keep the bottoms of pots and pans from being blackened by the flame of the wood fire, but they were sometimes removed to allow the flame to make direct contact with the pot or skillet to increase heat and decrease cooking time. The eyes could also be removed to add fuel (wood) to the fire.

The other room was used for everything else—sleeping, visiting, studying—everything. We slept three to a bed on the two full-sized beds in that room. I shared a bed with my two brothers. Charles was a bedwetter. The discomfort of sharing a small bed with two other people was often exacerbated on nights when Charles had accidents. Waking up with my night clothes and bed linens soaked and reeking with the odor of pee was never fun but was especially miserable on cold winter nights.

In lieu of a modern-day bathroom, we had a crude little outhouse about fifty yards from the house—a rickety little shelter that housed a bench-like platform with a hole in the center. Lying beside the hole was a Sears and Roebuck catalog or stack of other catalogues, magazines, or junk mail that served as our toilet paper. The annual Sears and Roebuck catalog was a huge, heavy, thick book containing hundreds of slick pages and was delivered by mail. It was published by one of the first department store chains to offer revolving credit—a concept that was embraced by many because it allowed people to make purchases and pay out over time. To further encourage wealthy people to buy from the mail order giant and poor people to live beyond their means, sale books and specialized publications were delivered throughout the year. Boy, were we excited when those sales catalogues came in the mail, especially the Christmas publication of the Sears and Roebuck catalogue dubbed the "Wish Book" with page after page of everything you could imagine: clothing, tools, TOYS, appliances, gizmos, and gadgets. We could not afford to make large purchases, but boy, could we dream, imagining ourselves riding on fancy scooters or replacing our cane fishing poles with rods and reels. Those same pages that inspired lofty hopes, dreams, and wishes served a dual purpose—first to allow us to let our imaginations soar, then to keep our hineys clean.

    My mother was a stickler for cleanliness, so we always kept a "wash pan" filled with water just outside the back door alongside an open water bucket. She called this nook the gallery. On a nail in the wall of the back porch near the water bucket hung a dipper crafted from a hollowed out long-stemmed gourd. There was only one dipper that was shared by all who had the need to quench their thirst while working or playing outdoors. No one dared to come into the house after an outhouse visit without first thoroughly washing his or her hands. I don't know which season was worse when it came to outhouse visits—the summer when the horrendous stench in that stuffy little building was amplified by the humid Arkansas heat or the winter when the wash pan water was so agonizingly frigid it caused my hands to throb.

As a child, I had never seen a toothbrush or heard of toothpaste. However, my mother's demands regarding personal hygiene were rigid. Her standards were high with no room for negotiation. My mother had a wise old aunt who shared her obsession for cleanliness and who, like my mother, was very smart and resourceful. The aunt discovered a homemade device that worked very well for scrubbing teeth. Once she shared that discovery with my mother, it became a part of our daily routines.

The first step was to cut a small branch, six to eight inches long, from a black gum sapling. Experience taught us that the branch had to be from a black gum tree. A sweet gum cutting would not work. The next step was to strip the branch, removing all leaves and any growths. Then, the larger end of the branch had to be soaked in water until it softened. Next, the softened end of the branch had to be chewed causing it to fray and create a brush-like device that was practical and effective for scrubbing teeth. Our toothpaste was made by dumping a teaspoon or so of baking soda into the palm of one hand. Using the wet, frayed end of our black gum toothbrush, we stirred the soda which made a paste that tasted horrible but worked very well to keep our chompers clean and pearly white. This is just one example of how we used the resources available to us in the backwoods of rural Arkansas to accomplish tasks that were much simpler for those who could afford to purchase things that we did not even know existed.

Our two-room remote little cabin had numerous cracks in the pine shingle roof and an abundance of cracks in the log walls as well. In Arkansas, we got far more rain than snow. Thunderstorms and downpours often cropped up with little or no warning. I remember everyone in the house scurrying about gathering pots, pans, buckets—anything that could be used to catch the rainwater making its way through the roof. The log walls also had numerous cracks big enough to see daylight through. Just as our poorly constructed roof offered only minimal protection from rain, the log walls gave little relief from extreme temperatures and allowed outside elements and creatures to enter our home.

I do not recall any efforts ever being made to patch the cracks in the roof. I do, however, remember my mother persistently working to seal the cracks in the walls. Every two weeks, a Grit newspaper (hailed "America's Greatest Family Newspaper") was delivered to rural homes by schoolboys who were allowed to keep a few pennies for each ten-cent paper they sold and delivered—usually by bicycle. After skimming and reading the parts of the fourteen-page magazine that were interesting, Mother used the separated pages of the publication to stuff into the cracks between the logs to help keep dust, scorpions, ants (aints, as we called them), and other creepy-crawly critters from gaining easy entry into our home. The hot, humid weather and stagnant water common in the wooded areas near our home were the perfect breeding grounds for mosquitoes the size of hummingbirds. I don't think cement spackling would have kept those bloodsuckers out of our home. Certainly, the pages of those Grit magazines did not. Almost ninety years later, I can still vividly remember the discomfort caused by insects and creatures that penetrated those walls.

I've heard folks say, "If these walls could talk . . ." In my case, I would add, "and if those cookstove eyes could talk about the things they saw." I can only imagine the topics that were discussed in that tiny kitchen. I'm also sure those eyes saw actions and interactions that we kids were protected from witnessing. Let there be no doubt that those old log walls and cast-iron stove eyes could share some fascinating stories that would run the gamut from funny and entertaining to brutal and heartbreaking.

A story I heard many times was about an incident that happened in 1937 when I was two years old. Food was scarce in our neck of the woods. I don't know if we still had Grandpaw's nanny goat, but I do wonder what she was fed if we did. My father had been away working in the East Texas oilfields where he met and made friends with a co-worker. When the job played out, Dad returned home to our old log house and his family. Much to his surprise, a few weeks after Dad's return, the friend from the oil fields showed up on our doorstep.

Questions flooded Dad's mind. What is this man doing here? How in the world did he find me in this God-forsaken place? Mom got busy and built a fire in the cookstove and heated the oven to make cornbread. She heated our big iron skillet on the stovetop to make cornmeal gravy—a staple in the homes of frugal Southern cooks struggling to feed their families and stretch limited food. I was told there was nothing else to eat or to offer our unexpected guest.

However, our lack of food did not hinder my mother from extending hospitality to our house guest and joyfully sharing what little we had. I am guessing the man had to sleep on the floor that night. The next morning, Mom was up early to make coffee. The menu for breakfast was the same as it had been the night before for supper—cornbread and cornmeal gravy. After the morning meal while Mom and Dad were occupied with the children, their guest slipped out the back and disappeared into the deep woods that surrounded our home, never to be seen again.

During my growing up years, the Great Depression had taken its toll. Lots of folks struggled just to get by, but my family was worse off than most because my father was such a poor provider. At a young age, I assumed the responsibility of doing all I could to help my mother keep food on the table.

Performing daily chores was also a necessity. Every member of the family had to pitch in, although not equally. Washday duties never changed. Unless rain, sickness, or some other unforeseen eventuality occurred, Monday was the dreaded designated washday. My older brother and I started early in the morning carrying water from a nearby spring to fill the tubs and pot used for doing laundry. Our father eventually installed a hand-operated pump that made the water job a little easier for us, but all those buckets of water still had to be filled and carried to the tubs and pot.

Charles and I had to carry enough water for two number three tubs, each of which had to be half filled. One was for washing clothes and linens in lye soap, the other for rinsing. In addition to the two laundry tubs, there was a big ol' black wash pot used for boiling blue jeans, overalls, and sometimes coveralls in soapy water—a type of pre-washing to prepare heavily soiled items for the rubboard process. I had the additional job of gathering wood for the fire under that big black pot.

Sometimes folks use the terms overalls and coveralls interchangeably, but they are actually two distinct types of garments. Overalls are basically trousers with an attached bib and galluses (shoulder straps). Coveralls, on the other hand, are a loose-fitting, one-piece outer garment to be worn over regular clothes. They literally cover the whole body from the neck down. Coveralls worn in the spring and summer are made of light-weight fabric and are worn primarily to protect the clothing underneath. Winter coveralls, on the other hand, are made of heavier fabric and are often lined with fleece or insulated for warmth. Laundry day was always dreaded, but even more so when winter coveralls had to be laundered. They were so bulky that only one pair could be boiled at a time. They were difficult to wring out and took hours to dry. They often had to be left hanging on the clothesline overnight because they did not dry completely before nightfall.

The actual laundering was women's work. While the jeans, overalls, and coveralls boiled, the women's washday routine started with the rubboard which was a thinly constructed board, approximately two by three feet, with short legs and a metal or glass surface designed to fit in a washtub and lean against its edge permitting the "washer woman" to rub the clothes up and down the corrugated surface to loosen dirt and muck. I remember my mother's knuckles bleeding during this phase of washday.

The next step was to rinse the clothes which had to be hand-wrung and then hung on a clothesline—a heavy wire strung about six feet off the ground between two trees. Clothespins were used to clip clothing and linens in place on the line to prevent hefty breezes or strong gusts of wind from carrying them away. Heavier clothes were hung on the fence. Because washday was so time consuming and physically exhausting, food for wash day was prepared the day before.

One night after one of those grueling all-day washdays, a most memorable experience occurred. I was all of nine years old at the time. My father was away working in another part of the state as he did quite often, leaving his wife and children to fend for themselves. We were all—my older brother, older sister, younger brother, and mother—dog tired and had just settled down for sleep when there was an unusual and startling noise outside. The strange sound pierced the silence of the night. We lived deep in the woods, so night noises were uncommon. This was a sound like none we had ever heard.

Startled by the disturbance, we all sat straight up in our beds—wide eyed, scared to death, and not moving a muscle. Moonlight filtered into our room through the cracks in the roof so that we could see one another's silhouettes. We waited in silence for a clue as to what that gosh-awful clamoring had been. I suspect we were all hoping our imaginations had gotten the best of us after a long, exhausting day. As we all held our breath, you could have heard a pin drop. If the silence lasted for another moment or two, my mom would have likely assured us that the unusual sound was nothing to be concerned about, told us to lay back down, and insisted that we wait until the light of morning to investigate. Then that unfamiliar sound happened again. This time, much louder leaving no doubt that something or someone was threatening our safety. As if expertly choreographed, we all simultaneously bailed onto the floor of that old shanty like a team of synchronized swimmers. We huddled behind one of the beds. Boy, were we ever terrified!

Somebody had to do something. We couldn't just sit there. Mustering all the courage a nine-year-old boy is capable of conjuring up, I grabbed Daddy's twelve-gauge shotgun and headed for the back door in the direction of the frightening commotion. One by one, my mother and three siblings fell in line behind me. Single file, our little parade cautiously approached the door— one soft, silent, tiptoe step at a time. You could have heard a mouse pee on a rug as I quietly and methodically maneuvered the back door completely open.

It was a dark, cloudy night, but the moon occasionally peeked through the clouds giving just enough illumination to identify objects in our backyard by their shadowy shapes. I could make out the figure of a man near a pine tree and could see that he was moving—swaying slightly from side to side but not coming forward toward our cabin. I called out to him and asked him to identify himself and tell us what his business was. He said nothing but continued to shuffle in place, remaining silent under that pine tree. I called out again—this time a little louder, demanding that he identify himself. Again, no reply. Dead silence. I was still terrified, but was getting a little mad, too—not the best combination of emotions for a terrified kid with a loaded shotgun. I really didn't want to shoot a man, but I was aware that my family was depending solely on me to protect them. I made a quick decision to give the intruder one last chance.

In the manliest voice I could muster, I called out loudly one last time threatening the man under the pine tree. "If you don't state your name and step out of the shadows right now, I am going to blow a damn hole clean through you."

My older brother then hollered, "Shoot the son of a b----."

About that time, the clouds covering the moon parted, giving all of us a clear view of the bandit. A gentle gust of wind rustled Daddy's freshly washed coveralls that Mom had hung on the clothesline a few hours earlier. We were all so relieved and so full of pent-up terror that we instantly burst out laughing hysterically as we watched Daddy's coveralls, firmly tethered to the clothesline, dance in place to the rhythm of the wind. You talk about some old-fashioned rejoicing! I don't know how long we sashayed around in the moonlight—hugging, slapping each other on the backs, and celebrating that there was no deranged invader trying to harm us. Boy, was I happy that I hadn't blown a hole through Daddy's best coveralls!

We were all very relieved, but now we were all also even more exhausted than we had been the first time our heads hit our pillows earlier that evening. We all fell asleep quickly without giving the unusual noise that started the whole charade another thought. The next morning, we discovered our old hound dog on our back porch with his head firmly lodged in a scrap bucket. No doubt he was the culprit who had been blindly batting around just outside our back door in the middle of the night trying to free himself of the unwanted helmet and creating dreadful noises that were quite unfamiliar to us.

Both food and firewood were scarce in our household. We never seemed to have quite enough of either. Since the only fuel for both heating and cooking was wood, someone had to be responsible for making sure there was a constant and plentiful supply. My family did not own land, so we had to cut oak trees using a rusty old crosscut saw from property that belonged to other people. As far back as memory takes me, my older brother and I were in charge of cutting, hauling, and splitting wood. I am not sure who had that job before Charles and I reached the ages of eight and nine and took on the chore, but I am certain it was not my father. I suspect the chore fell on my mother and Grandpaw.

I vividly remember a cold winter night when Dad returned after another of his stints of working away from home for a long period of time. When he came through the door, he announced that he had a present for Charles and me. He then presented us with a shiny new crosscut saw. Charles and I whooped and hollered as we danced a jig. It didn't dawn on us that the shiny, new, eight-foot crosscut saw was an instrument of work. Poor, dumb, "backwoodsey" boys.

A lot of our food came from hunting and fishing. The standard for most families in those days was three meals a day—breakfast, dinner, and supper. I used to tell my army buddies that I never missed a meal, but I postponed a few. Most of our suppers—the biggest meal of the day—consisted of a pot of beans or soup with fresh cornbread. We usually drank water with our meals, although tea was an occasional weekend treat. Our food was prepared on our wood cook stove. My brother and father were skilled hunters and fishermen, thus providing most of the protein we consumed. They could both shoot the eye out of a squirrel. My skill level in those aspects never quite measured up to theirs.

I did, though, have a knack for listening in on "grown-up talk." I recall my grandparents having conversations when they thought no one else was listening. They often talked about what "poor money managers and providers" my parents were—especially my father. Because of my keen eavesdropping skills, I learned that my grandparents' opinion of my father's poor resource management was shared by my aunts and uncles on both sides of the family. Their criticism was shocking and hurtful to me when I was a youngster. I still adored my parents and believed they did no wrong. As I grew older and wiser, I began to comprehend the judgments to the contrary.

Neither of our parents imposed many rules or restrictions on us kids other than to abide by the "do right" rule. They did not seem to concern themselves with what we were doing as long as we were not bothering them and were doing well enough in school to pass from one grade to the next each year. Those conditions were perfect for us knuckle-headed boys who could spend endless hours entertaining ourselves by hunting, fishing, or playing in the woods, but our sister found our lifestyle frustrating and unfulfilling. She was eager to finish school and move away.

Leisure activities consisted mainly of playing whatever games our imaginations conjured up, visiting with family or neighbors, telling and retelling stories, and irregularly attending church. We did have an old battery-operated radio that had to be "rigged" to play. Dad used to bring the battery from his old Plymouth pickup truck into the house—usually only on Friday nights when New York boxing was on. Dad was a huge fan of heavy-weight boxing. He always rooted for Billy Conn, but Conn just could not defeat Joe Lewis. Dad always got upset and accused the referees of cheating. Maybe the first time I got an inkling that we were poor was when I learned that some families had a separate battery for their home radios and that their automobile batteries stayed in their cars or trucks. There were even some people who were so rich that they owned long-lasting factory-made batteries. Wow!

A story that was told countless times in our home and that was funnier each time I heard it proves that there is a God who takes care of little children. Once every few weeks, my whole family would get all gussied up in our best clothes and go to church in Dad's ragged old 1938 Plymouth pickup. Mom, Dad, and my sister, Mary Lou, rode in the cab while we three boys were relegated to the bed of the truck. Charles and I usually stood with our arms resting on the top of the cab facing forward as we bumped and bobbled down the crude dirt road.

One particular Sunday afternoon, Keith, who was about four years old at the time, chose to sit on the side of the pickup bed for the ride home. Dad was a good driver, but almost always drove too fast for conditions on those old roads. Because it had rained for several days that week, the road was muddier and slicker than usual with water standing in ruts and ditches. As Dad glided around a familiar curve, the rear end of the truck slid one way, and Keith flew off the edge of the pickup bed in the opposite direction. His little body bounced off the rear fender then careened into a water-filled ditch. Charles and I (ages eleven and ten respectively) started frantically pounding on the top of the cab and hollering for Dad to stop. We were certain Keith was dead or at least seriously injured. As Dad slammed on the brakes, Keith bounced up out of that mudhole like a jack-in-the-box.

Soaked to the bone and covered with mud, he came running behind us yelling, "Hey, wait for me!"

The old truck finally skidded to a stop, and we saw that by God's grace and Keith's good fortune of landing on his buttocks in a soft-bottomed ditch, he was virtually unscathed. Our father immediately launched into one of his infamous tirades, blaming everyone except himself for the accident. Charles, Mary Lou, and

I laughed all the way home. For years, we teased Keith about that incident. We often told him that he wasn't the same after that fall or that he was still addled from that Sunday afternoon tumble.

Other than my grandparents, we did not have a lot of visitors, but there was one neighbor I will never forget—an intrusive, abrasive woman who took no pride in personal hygiene. My mother was a God-fearing woman who taught us right and wrong according to the Word and typically modeled those standards, but Mom would bend the truth a tad when this uninvited visitor came calling. The woman was always filthy. My mother was intolerant of uncleanliness and was always frustrated when this unkempt woman came calling. The nasty neighbor always asked to "borrow" something—usually our ice cream freezer. Mother would spin a tale on a dime to keep her wares at home and send the unwelcome guest away empty-handed.

Another memory that made quite an impression on my young mind was that of a somewhat ordinary occurrence. Perhaps the reason it has stayed with me all these years is that my father rarely admitted being wrong or acknowledged when he made a mistake. He always blamed others or made excuses. The incident happened one evening when my father had been sitting and reading his Bible while Mother cooked supper.

When she had the meal ready to serve, she announced, "Dinner is ready."

Dad got up, opened the back door, and called out, "Keith, where art thou?" He immediately realized what he had done and looked around to see if anyone had heard him unintentionally use Bible language to summon Keith for supper. We three children could not contain ourselves although we knew Dad was apt to go into a rage if he realized we were laughing at him. Regardless, we couldn't help ourselves and began to laugh and holler, making sport of our father's slip of the tongue. Surprisingly, our father got tickled and started laughing, too. Our entire family shared a rare and joyful moment of laughing and dancing around as we made light of one of my father's mistakes, something that he rarely acknowledged, let alone found amusing.

By the time I was fifteen, I had developed a love and talent for baseball. Whenever I could make the seven-mile trip from Fenter to Poyen for the weekend, it was baseball, baseball, baseball all weekend except for church time. Poyen was where my siblings and I attended school and the home of my maternal grandmother which is where I stayed during my baseball weekends.

Baseball was a game I fell in love with. Weighing in at only slightly more than one hundred pounds and having a short wheelbase, I was not well-suited for some sports. However, baseball was something I could do well with my physical stature. It became my passion. I became better and better at America's favorite pastime. I was quick as a cricket and had an arm like Carl Furillo. I was pretty darn good for a little fellow.

One Sunday afternoon just before a big game was about to start, Bill Stenson, an older friend of mine, sidled up next to me and whispered, "See that man over there? He asked me to point you out to him. He's a scout for the Detroit Tigers." Bill went on to tell me that the scout was from Memphis, Tennessee, and that he had driven four hours just to watch me play. Wow!

Soon, the big-league scout came over to where I was standing and introduced himself to me. He made small talk then pushed up the right sleeve of my jersey. He thanked me and then mumbled something that was inaudible before disappearing into the crowd of spectators.

If I remember correctly, I made a couple of sparkling plays at shortstop ala Pee Wee Reese. I got three good hits, one of which was a triple. Then, just to show out, I stole home plate—a play that is no longer permitted and one I copied from Jackie Robinson. I was having a heck of a game. During the sixth inning, I asked my friend where the scout was.

Bill lowered his head and said in a low tone, "He left just before the game started."

Just like that, my hope of replacing Pee Wee Reese as the Dodger shortstop was completely dashed. Like so many aspiring young athletes, I had to get realistic about my future. Shortly after graduation and a week after I turned eighteen, I joined the U.S. Paratroopers.

Meet the Family

My mother, Chloe Walker Miller, was an angel among us. Despite hardships and poor health, her faith in God never wavered. Although her formal education ended in the sixth grade, she was highly intelligent and instilled in all her children a love for learning and a drive to be successful in life. She was determined that her children would create lives for themselves that would surpass the quality of life she experienced in the backwoods of that small rural setting where opportunities were limited, and resources were scarce. What our father lacked in ambition and dedication to his family, our mother compensated for with ingenuity and grit. She devoted her life to caring for her family, working from daylight to dark every day to ensure that she met every need of her children that was within her ability.

My father, Harry Miller, was a complicated man. He was a tall, slender, charismatic redhead with a ready smile. He was well-known and well-liked by members of the church and the Poyen community. My father's public persona was that of a fine Christian husband and father. In stark contrast, the Harry Miller who was "head of our household" was abusive and neglectful. Grandpaw did his best to teach my father how to be a good provider. Grandpaw led by example, but those lessons did not take. My father never took responsibility for his family's lack of food and necessities. As far back as I can remember, he blamed Charles and me for being lazy and irresponsible when our wood supply was insufficient. It was not unusual for my father to travel long distances and make great sacrifices for others while we struggled at home and sometimes did without. While our dad was quick to come to the aid of others, he disregarded the needs of his family. He was the kind of man who would give the shirt off his back to a stranger while his own wife and children lacked bare necessities. The charm and generosity he extended to others was rarely shared with us.

My father never had a bank account, rather he kept all his money in his pockets. He was a master automobile mechanic and heavy machinery operator. Despite earning good wages, he was always broke. Family members often questioned where all of Harry's money went. Of course, no one dared to ask him directly because everyone lived in fear of him and his unpredictable angry outbursts. We all wondered but never, to this day, knew what ol' Harry Miller did with all his money. What we did know was that he did not spend it on his wife and children.

Like most young boys, I looked up to and idolized my father. I tended to ignore or minimize his shortcomings including his sometimes harsh, abusive behaviors. His presence in our home was typically accompanied by tension and anxiety because of his unpredictable and explosive nature. Dad often lost his temper and struck our mother with his fists. We kids begged him to stop but learned that if we dared try to intervene, he would turn on us. None of us were a physical match for our father, so all we could do was watch helplessly and pray that he would stop striking our mother before seriously injuring her.

Harry Miller never apologized for anything. I have no memory of him ever saying, "I'm sorry." When he calmed down after a fit of rage, he returned to his "normal" self and expected everyone else to do the same. Perhaps the single incident that totally crushed any lingering admiration I had for my father occurred during the time he was serving as Sunday school superintendent at the local Baptist church. I do not recall what my younger brother did to trigger our father's rage, but I do remember that Dad took Keith down an old dirt road and beat him mercilessly. When Keith emerged from the woods, his blue jeans were shredded and glued to his skin by his own blood. The rose-colored glasses through which I had viewed my father until that day were shattered.

I choose not to divulge other instances of my father's brutality. They would be too laborious to endure. Suffice to say, I learned that the love a boy has for his father can be destroyed. Totally disillusioned about my father, I became aware of Harry Miller's selfish actions that eventually became impossible to conceal from others. His reckless money management earned him the reputation of a "debt beater."

He became an alcoholic and lost the respect of most of the members of our church—something that he had coveted so much in previous years. The man that I once revered as charming, strong, and tough and who had been held in high esteem by his peers disintegrated into a weak and pathetic drunk. Our family was embarrassed and humiliated by the disgrace of a man my father became.

My older brother, Charles, was the smartest of the Miller children. He always made straight A's in every subject. In many ways, he took after our father who was also very intelligent. Charles got my father's brains and followed in his footsteps, exhibiting both the best and worst of our father's attributes. Like our father, Charles became a very skilled hunter and fisherman. He was also a whiz at games and consistently won against peers and adults alike. I loved my other two siblings dearly, but I freely admit that Charles was my favorite. We were inseparable until we reached the ages of about fourteen and fifteen.

My brother changed dramatically. Charles became more of an introvert, and I was the polar opposite. He started running with other boys, excluding and shunning me to the point of being rude, even cruel at times. I made the mistake of "courting up" to Charles attempting to regain favor with him—something I continued to do well into adulthood. I was in my fifties before my sweet Emma convinced me of the futility of my efforts to win my brother's affection. We recognized that at the core of my brother's negative outlook on life and unkind words and actions toward me was self-loathing. I tried for decades to help him see his worth. With Emma's help, I eventually accepted that I could not force my brother to see himself through my lenses nor could I persuade him to allow me to have a seat at his table.

Despite his intelligence and natural talents, he became an alcoholic driven by jealousy and bitterness. He earned a meager wage working as a clerk for Malvern Brick and Tile for many years until his alcoholism cost him his job. Charles died in 2012 at the age of seventy-nine. Only God knows why my brother made such a dramatic change during his teen years that started him on a collision course with life. I will love him dearly until the day I die and will forever cherish the precious memories of the closeness and good times we once shared.

My sister, Mary Lou, was the first-born child and only daughter of Harry and Chloe Miller. She was as beautiful as she was intelligent—tall and curvy with a perfectly shaped face. She looked identical to a beautiful movie star of the time, Lee Ann Remick. Just recently one of my old high school friends said to me, "Mary Lou was the most beautiful girl ever in Grant County." I agreed with his assessment of my sister. As an adult, Mary Lou confessed to me that being the only girl with three brothers had been challenging for her. She did not enjoy hunting, fishing, or cutting wood. There was little for a young lady who was not a tomboy to do where we lived.

Mary Lou graduated as valedictorian of her class and left home the following week. She moved to San Antonio where she married a handsome older man, Pat, who shared some of our father's flaws. He was, on the surface, charming and kind. However, beneath his public façade was a deceptive man with an explosive temper. Gradually, his true colors surfaced. It came to light that he was much older than he had led Mary Lou to believe and that he had been married at least two times before. Pat and Mary Lou had two sons, Anthony and Ronald, who were born two years apart. Eventually, the marriage ended in divorce, and Pat abandoned his family. At the age of forty-one, Mary Lou and her older son who was twenty-one at the time, were killed along with four others, in a tragic train and automobile collision in 1974 in Schertz, Texas, just outside of San Antonio.

Ronald, Mary Lou's surviving son, became like a son to Emma and me. We supported him in every way we could. He became an amazing man, earning a master's degree in education as well as a degree in nursing. He raised two children who are sweet and productive adults. Ron, who refers to Emma and me as his mom and dad, calls us Papaw and Jugi as our grandchildren do. He still lives in San Antonio and makes the one-hour drive to Austin almost every Sunday for breakfast and an all-day visit with us. My sister would be so very proud of her son and grandchildren.

Keith, the baby of the family, continued to live at home until he was drafted into the U.S. Army at the age of twenty-six. He eventually married and had three sons. Keith chose a path of self-destruction. He eventually hit rock bottom when he deserted his wife and children to move in with a high school senior and her parents. He suffered a fatal heart attack at the age of forty-eight.

At the ripe old age of seventeen, I graduated with eight fellow classmates from Poyen High School. I had to wait a few months after graduation before I could enlist in the United States Army because the minimum age for enlistment was eighteen. It was during the enlistment process that I first became painfully aware of how the comedy of errors made by that backwoods physician who filled out my birth certificate in 1935 would impact my life. His reckless errors were discovered by my Army recruiting officer and delayed my swearing in. Finally, on October 6, 1953, —two weeks after my first introduction to military life—I became a private in the U.S. Army. I was the first person on either side of my family to enlist in the military.

I served a total of three years in the military. I was an Army Ranger and a member of the 101st Airborne Division. I became a Korean War veteran with thirty-one parachute jumps including five that were overseas and two that were confidential. At the age of eighteen, I bought Mother and Daddy the only home they ever owned. It was a charming three-bedroom country home in the town of Poyen where they lived for the last twenty-nine years of their lives. Dad made positive life changes that lasted about ten years. He joined the Baptist church just two city blocks from Mother's pretty white house. He eventually started drinking again. Alcoholism, once again, took hold of his life and never loosened its grip until his death.

When Mother began to have health issues characterized by decreased strength and stamina, her local doctor discovered a heart condition she was born with and that had gone undetected all her life. In 1960, when my mother was forty-nine years old, her health deteriorated significantly. Her heart condition worsened to the extent that local doctors said she would likely die within months without an operation. Her only hope of survival was open-heart surgery—a procedure that was not unheard of at that time, but one that was in its infancy and certainly not routinely performed in our part of the world.

At the time of my mother's health crisis, I was twenty-five years old. Emma and I had been married three years, and I was in my final year of college. We had no children at the time. When my mom engaged in her battle for life, Emma and I had to square off against my father and older brother who vehemently opposed my mother having surgery. Emma and I used every resource available to us to ensure that my mother got the best medical care available.

We discovered that there was a young Japanese surgeon, Dr. Masauki Hara, who was being hailed as a pioneer in the field of open-heart surgery and who was working at University of Arkansas Medical Center in, believe it or not, Little Rock, Arkansas. Boy, were we hopeful and highly motivated to explore the possibility of my mother getting a shot at the life-saving procedure! Further inquiries revealed that the cost of the operation was astronomical—more than I would ever be able to beg, borrow, or steal. Discouraged but not yet defeated, I soon discovered a ray of hope. I learned that if I could persuade our county judge to declare that my parents were paupers and sign a specific document to that effect, the State of Arkansas would cover the cost of the operation, and my mother would be able to have the surgery at no cost to her or her family.

It was a hard-fought battle, but Emma and I eventually won my father and brother over. We jumped through all the hoops necessary to get Mother set up for surgery. When we met with Dr. Hara, he was straightforward and told us that the surgery was very complicated and risky with about a fifty-percent success rate. Those odds sounded pretty good considering that her chances of living more than a short time without it were nil. For three days following the extensive surgery, my mother had to lay on an ice cot to keep her blood flow and heart rate as low as possible without stopping her heart completely. Recovery was slow and grueling, but Mother survived. She later said that the three days on the ice cot were, by far, the worst part of the whole ordeal. She even said that she would rather die than endure that excruciating pain again. Nonetheless, that high-risk operation allowed my mother to enjoy another eighteen years of life.

Because of my military service, I was able to attend college—the plan I developed in my senior year of high school. I was twenty-one years old and in my first year of college when I met and eloped with my sweet Emma. Our first baby, Mona Marie, went to heaven as an infant. We subsequently had two beautiful and healthy daughters, Leticia Lea and Michelle Evette, who have given us four amazing grandchildren. What blessings!

At the age of eighty-five and after having lived all those years in Arkansas, Emma and I moved to Autin, Texas, accepting an invitation from our younger daughter, Michelle, who had become a highly regarded federal prosecutor in Austin with western Texas as her jurisdiction. She wanted her aging parents nearby so she could help care for them, and we now call Austin home. Emma and I are enjoying our golden years and are using much of our time to reminisce and write about the amazing life we have shared for the last sixty-seven years.

Now that I have introduced some of the most significant people in my growing up years and given a brief overview of my life, I will share a few stories of the many experiences and adventures that have molded me. Collectively, those life events have allowed me to experience every emotion imaginable. Some brought me to tears; others still make me laugh out loud every time I think about them. All have woven together to create the tapestry that is my life and to put me on a path that has led me to the place of contentment I now enjoy. I can honestly say that if I had my life to live over again, I would not change a thing.

Let's Talk Military

Because I was only seventeen when I graduated from high school in May 1953, I had to wait until I turned eighteen the following September to begin serving in the Army. My eighteenth birthday brought with it all the rights and privileges of adulthood with one exception—the right to vote. That liberty required a person to be twenty-one years old and to pay a two-dollar poll tax. I found it puzzling that at eighteen I could join the military and go to war for my country but could not cast a vote for my commander in chief. The stories of my military experiences are too numerous to tell all of them, but I will share some of the highlights.

While in the military, I had the good fortune to be under the command of two of the most magnificent men I have ever known: Sergeant Nathaniel Lamirande and Captain Paul Lavendar. Both men were tough but fair and truly cared about their subordinates. I developed a special bond with each of them and grew to love and respect Sgt. Lamirande and Capt. Lavendar more than any of the men in my own family. At the age of eighty-nine, I feel that I can boast a bit. In truth, although I was the youngest of nearly two hundred paratroopers—a rugged, tough bunch—I prided myself on being one of the most highly trained and skilled of their soldiers.

Four decades after serving together in the U.S. Army, each of them confirmed that truth.

Although the Army was a means to an end for me, I took advantage of every opportunity to learn new skills during those three years of service. I completed basic training; large-truck driving school; small arms care, firing and safety training; paratrooper jump school; and Army Ranger School. Twice, I was asked to consider Officer Candidate School (OCS).

Not long after joining the U.S. Army, a major summoned me to his orderly room (a room in the military that is used for administrative purposes). I arrived early because I was afraid not to. I had no idea why a major had summoned me. When I was called into his plush office, the major got right to the point. He had my military file in front of him and informed me that my high entrance exam results qualified me for OCS. Before I had a chance to respond, he paused while thumbing through my file and said, "I just noticed that you are too young for OCS. You are dismissed."

I soon learned that paratroopers, hailed as "an unusually tough group with pride to boot," earned extra "hazard pay" because of the risks that came with their assignments. I was attracted to this group for two reasons: (1) I was a bit of a scrapper and had earned the reputation of being pretty tough myself, and (2) the extra hazard pay—fifty-five dollars each month—would allow me to purchase the only house my parents ever owned which I did at the age of eighteen.

Not long after finishing "jump school," I received orders to spend a day guarding twenty of our own prisoners, each of whom had violated some Army code. I was handed a twelve-gauge shotgun along with several buckshot shells and instructed to shoot any prisoner who left the boundary of the restricted area. The evening before this dreaded assignment, I initiated a conversation with a veteran corporal. I told him about my orders and confided in him that I could not shoot a fellow American. His knowing grin communicated, "Me neither." As a veteran, he had been in my shoes several times and offered this young soldier some sage advice.

He said, "If you have a prisoner break and run, aim well over his head and fire. Nine times out of ten, he will stop and return. Keep the spent shell as proof that you fired and missed."

I then asked, "If one of those suckers does get away, will I really have to take his place as I was told?"

The old vet replied, "Probably not, but I really don't know."

Bright and early the next day, my barely eighteen-year-old self, armed with a twelve-gauge shotgun and a handful of buckshot shells, took twenty prisoners and supervised them as they worked hard all morning cutting and trimming grass in sweltering heat. At about

10:00 a.m., I thought it was time for those hot and sweaty boys to take a break and water up. I told them to gather on a grassy knoll near where they had been working and to sit close together. They complied and everything was going without a hitch until a helicopter suddenly appeared overhead.

This extremely loud distraction created a perfect opportunity for an escape, but thank God, every single prisoner stayed put. We all watched without moving expecting the 'copter to move on. But no. That rascal sat down right there beside us. The rear door of that bird opened and out jumped a sergeant with enough confetti (stripes) on his sleeves to burn a dead mule. He immediately called the prisoners to attention and gave an order I had never heard.

"Uncover."

Obviously, the command was not unfamiliar to the prisoners because every one of them, in unison, snapped their flimsy caps off. In my peripheral vision, I saw a second person bale out of the 'copter. When I realized our second guest was a two-star general tromping straight toward me in an angry manner, I started trembling. Thank the Heavenly Father I remembered how an officer of any rank was to be saluted when one of lower rank was carrying a gun or rifle. I snapped sharply to attention and saluted the major general who asked gruffly if I was in charge.

"Yes, sir." I replied.

Then all hell broke loose. That highly ranked officer made the incorrect assumption that the prisoners had been lounging in the shade all morning instead of doing hard labor and that I had allowed them to do so. He did not give me a chance to explain, and I knew better than to interrupt his tirade.

The other officer, who was a sergeant, took over command of my twenty boys as the major general thoroughly berated me. I stood at attention, as did the prisoners, the whole time and never blinked or uttered a syllable. I was thinking that perhaps the major general and his wife must have gotten drunk and fought the whole night before. Why else would a superior officer behave in a manner so inconsistent with his rank? Finally, the general seemed to run out of steam and motioned for the sergeant to board the helicopter, but not before instructing him to get my name, serial number, and address as well as my commander's name, organization, and location.

I had never been more intimidated, but those twenty prisoners did not seem to be shaken in the least. Having been soldiers before becoming prisoners, some of them had likely guarded prisoners just as I was doing that day. Fortunately, they remained respectful and in control of their emotions until the helicopter ascended and faded out of sight, but they could not keep it together another second longer. They all simultaneously broke out into the most booming fits of laughter I had ever seen or heard. They howled for several minutes, holding their sides and slapping each other's backs. Those boys found the whole incident much more hilarious than their shotgun-wielding guard did.

I knew I needed to get to my captain before the general did, but when I returned from my assignment late that evening, Capt. Lavendar and Sgt. Lamirande had already left for the day. I didn't sleep much, if any, that night and was up early the next morning awaiting a signal from a buddy of mine who had agreed to let me know the minute my superiors arrived. As soon as the signal was given, I hurried over to the orderly room and asked Sgt. Lamirande if I might speak to the captain. Lamirande suggested that I brief him first, which I did. He, like the prisoners, found the story amusing and laughed robustly as he escorted me to the captain. I still failed to see the humor in my situation.

Capt. Lavendar wanted to hear every detail about the incident. He grinned as I recounted the humiliating experience. The captain, too, seemed more amused than concerned. After hearing the whole story, he told me to take the day off because he could tell I had not slept. I did feel a sense of relief that neither of my superiors seemed overly concerned. The next day the captain sent for me and shared the battalion commander's response.

"Tell Pvt. Miller not to concern himself if a two-star general has nothing more to do than land his helicopter to chew out a young private." Was I ever relieved! This story is an unbiased truth and shows that truth is sometimes stranger than fiction.

I had more than a few fist fights while enlisted, but only one that resulted in disciplinary action. I had just been promoted to E-4 and had my new insignias sewn onto all my shirts and jackets. I was quite proud of my accomplishment. About that time, a sergeant (E-5) transferred in from a unit in Germany. He was a brawny, six-two bully who boasted of being a golden glove boxer. He and I immediately shared a mutual contempt for one another.

Shortly after his arrival, early one morning he ordered me to clean the latrine.

I replied, "No, Sergeant. I am an E-4, and E-4's do not work kitchens or clean latrines. That is an old rule in this outfit."

His response was, "My rule says you will."

Thinking the conversation was over, I turned my back and proceeded to walk away. Then that robust golden glove boxer made one of the biggest mistakes of his life. He forcefully shoved me through the latrine door. Instinctively, I spun around much like Willie Mays did when he made his historic "catch and throw" off Vic Wertz's bat in the 1954 World Series. My first punch relocated the tyrant's nose. Fueled by anger and adrenaline, I commenced to put a world of hurt on the addled old boy. I knew the price I would have to pay for the fight was going to be high, so I made sure I got my money's worth. My only hope was that the extra-large, power-tripping Goliath would be too embarrassed to report the altercation. That didn't happen. The super-sized snitch did not waste any time tattling to our superiors.

I soon found myself standing before the powers that be. I lied like a hound dog, but it really did no good. The fresh evidence (the sergeant's disfigured face) was too strong against me. The appointed prosecutor asked, "Miller, do you want to accept an Article 15 or go before the court?"

Having never faced a disciplinary action, I inquired about my options. The prosecutor explained that I could either consent to an Article 15 which meant I would put myself at his mercy and accept whatever punishment he deemed appropriate or opt for a court-martial before a panel of officers. I knew that if I went before the panel of officers, I would likely receive maximum punishment for striking a superior. Therefore, I chose the former.

I said, "I will accept an Article 15, Sir, and I ask for your mercy." I could read his face and knew that asking for mercy got his attention.

The prosecutor pushed a document in front of me and said, "Sign here, Private."

"Private? I am a Specialist E-4."

Immediately, the gravity of his words registered, and I fully comprehended what he was saying. That did not stop him from stating the obvious.

"Not anymore. You are now Private (E-1) again, and you will be confined, for the next fourteen days, to a restricted area that I will draw out for you." He went on to explain that if I broke that restriction by stepping one toe outside of the designated area that included only my living area and the mess hall, my fate would be out of his hands, and I would automatically go before a higher court. He said, "I can promise you that you will most likely be headed to prison if that occurs. Are we clear, Miller?"

"Yes, Sir."

Later that day I was all alone, laying on my bunk, when the door to the barracks opened and in walked a burly black soldier, well over six feet tall and weighing in at about two hundred twenty pounds. I didn't know him well but had developed a fondness for him the few times our paths had crossed and sensed that the feeling was mutual. All I knew about the man was that he was from Georgia and that he was known as "Charlie B." He entered with quick, light steps and headed straight toward me with his right arm outstretched for a handshake. I quickly sat up, shook his hand, and invited him to sit down. He declined, stating that he only had a minute.

With a hushed voice he said, "Johnny Reb (my nickname in the Army), that SOB that's making your life difficult right now is making threats, but don't you worry. We are taking care of him." While I was touched by his words, I could not allow him to put himself in jeopardy to defend me.

I said, "Charlie B, please don't get yourself in trouble. It will be much more difficult for you to get exonerated than it would be for a white boy."

Resolute, he repeated himself. "Johnny, Reb. Don't. You. Worry. I completely understand what you are saying, but we are brothers."

He did not give me the opportunity to say anything else. Charlie B spun around and headed back toward the door. A few tears trickled down my cheeks as I watched my brother leave.

Two days into my fourteen-day sentence, a siren like none of us had heard before blasted our area. Everyone was petrified. What in the world is that? We soon learned that the siren indicated a Red Alert which meant that everyone was to immediately change into full combat gear. Initially, we paratroopers thought that perhaps the Korean Truce had failed but quickly learned that this was actually the beginning of a two-week field exercise. As I was preparing for the mission, one of my good buddies came running up to me.

He was out of breath and practically panting as he said, "Johnny Reb, you better check out whether you can go. This assignment is outside of your designated area." Once again, one of my brothers had my back. It had not occurred to me that participating in the exercise would violate my order to stay within the designated area. I set out to find out what I should do.

The captain was in a high-level meeting, so Sgt. Lamirande had to handle the situation. He quickly gathered a few junior officers to make a judgement call. They unanimously agreed that I should stay put. I removed my combat gear and headed for my bunk as my fellow soldiers set out toward the rugged boondocks for a fourteen-day assignment. I felt a little guilty that I would have a nice warm bed and hot food while my fellow soldiers battled the elements. This was the moment I realized that my Article 15 was a blessing in disguise.

On the third day of the fourteen-day Red Alert exercise, the temperature suddenly dropped from around seventy degrees Fahrenheit to twenty-eight. The winter monsoon came a month early. Winter precipitation set in. Those boys were out there with no rain gear or winter clothing. Poor paratroopers! Our entire outfit, minus one, was cold, wet, and miserable. I thought about all the equipment and vehicles that were going to return covered with mud and how every inch of those things would have to be washed, rubbed, polished, and shined so that they could pass inspection before the exercise could officially end.

Then it hit me. "Oh! Ho! I am going to catch it when my buddies get back." Boy, did I!

Five days later Capt. Lavendar persuaded a high-ranking general to call off the exercise. I was elated for my buddies, but it was just the beginning of the harassment I was about to endure. It really wasn't as bad as it could have been. The thing I had dreaded most—being thrown into a cold shower—never happened. A few of the guys were extra salty and shunned me for a few days. My bunk got turned over once and I had to endure several days of "cat calls," but all that was nothing ol' Johnny Reb couldn't take in stride. A little time and a lot of camaraderie took care of everything. As for that transplanted sergeant (E-5), six days after he bit off more than he could chew with this five-six specialist (E-4), he was quietly transferred back to Germany from whence he came.

A few months later, Charlie B came to me and confided that he had contracted a venereal disease for the second time. He was afraid to seek treatment from the Army because after three times, a dishonorable discharge would be issued. My advice was for him to take a short furlough and to use that time to travel, dressed in civies, to a distant town and see a civilian doctor for treatment. He followed my guidance and thanked me many, many times even after we were both separated from military life.

As my fellow soldiers and I trudged through various rigid military schools and gradually transitioned from civilian kids to military fighting machines, we often heard tales of classified missions but seldom entertained any real notion of actually being involved in one. I was a member of a group of about forty highly trained youngsters eager for some "real men experience." We were just what the generals wanted—a group of eighteen- to twenty-year-olds not yet mature enough to recognize the dangers of the missions we hoped to be a part of. We became known as the "Rogue Group" and were led by a couple of "ninety-day wonders" whose experience in what we were doing was as limited as ours.

Our group was gyroscoped to Kyushu, Japan, in a C-123 airplane to replace the 187th Regimental Combat Team that was of equal status to ours. We were in an area known as Camp Wood that had been an officers' training camp for the Japanese during World War II. It was a nice compound with a major military airport only minutes away.

While we were stationed in Kyushu, Japan, our unit's mission was to stay poised to challenge any communist uprising in the Far East at a moment's notice. One pleasant weekend, some of my buddies and I applied for and received a long weekend pass. Entertainment options were limited for those who did not care to spend their spare time drinking. Our crew decided we would all take in a movie.

In addition to our unit of paratroopers, there was also a large attachment of regular Army troops in the area and a Navy base not far from Camp Wood. Any given weekend, the smelly old movie theater near the bases was packed with military men. The crowd gathered there on the day of my outing with my buddies included soldiers from different branches of the military. When assembled for weekend entertainment, all soldiers were eager to put responsibilities on the back burner for a few hours and just have a good time. Most of the movie goers were young men full of vim and vigor. The roar of the crowd talking and laughing while awaiting the beginning of the picture show was so loud I doubt that we would have heard a bomb drop. However, as soon as the first flicker of light appeared on the screen, a hush immediately fell over the crowd and the old theater became silent.

In those days, movies shown overseas started out with news and sports clips prior to the main attraction from the good ol' U.S. of A. My buddies and I, along with everyone else in the stuffy theater, were glued to the big screen hoping for a glimpse of a familiar landmark, familiar images of our favorite celebrities or sports heroes—anything to make us feel reconnected to our homeland. Much to my surprise, as the sports highlights were being played, up popped a picture of a tall, handsome basketball player who was making a name for himself in the sports world playing for the University of Kentucky. I immediately recognized the star on the screen as my cousin with whom I had grown up. I could not believe my eyes. Goodness gracious!

I was so overcome with excitement that I leapt up out of my seat and loudly proclaimed, "Hey, that's my cousin, Robert Burrow!"

Those words had hardly passed my lips when the sports commentator announced, "This six-eight center for Adloph Rupp has just been selected as 1954 player of the year."

Man, oh Man, was I ecstatic to the extent that I could not contain my enthusiasm. My buddies were quick to start a commotion that spread through the cinema. They razzed me with a barrage of insults—a common expression of comradery within the military community.

"Now, how tall are you, Miller? Five feet and seven inches? And this guy is supposed to be your cousin?"

Others who did not know me joined in, but not in the same good-humored manner as my seven or eight buddies. Everyone there was agitated by the disruption my outburst had caused.

Before long, everybody in the building was on their feet and shouting things like, "What the h--- is going on?" Eventually, the projectionist stopped the reel and attempted to contain the pandemonium that had broken out. The crowd could not be quieted.

I was keenly aware that my emotional response to seeing my cousin was the catalyst for the mayhem, but there was nothing I could say or do that would end the chaotic scene. The crowd was out of control. Finally, someone very intelligent, perhaps a manager or staff member, started playing the U.S. National Anthem. All the moviegoers were already on their feet. Immediately, every soldier in the room from different branches of the military became silent, promptly assumed proper stance, and saluted the flag until the last note of the anthem.

Order was restored. As I took my seat, I thought to myself, "This is one time in my life I wish I had kept my mouth shut." I later thought of that old Arkansas saying: "It is better to remain silent and be thought a fool than to speak and remove all doubt."

For most of the soldiers the chaotic scene of that night was quickly forgotten, but my buddies made sure the embarrassing story about my energetic display of emotion in the movie theater spread through our unit like wildfire. For weeks, I caught it from my fellow paratroopers. I was teased and harassed mercilessly about my claim of being a cousin to basketball great Robert Burrow whose number 50 jersey still hangs from the rafters of Rupp Arena in Lexington, Kentucky. Once again, truth is sometimes stranger than fiction.

My second invitation to OCS came while I was still stationed in Kyushu, Japan. I was summoned by a major in much the same way I had been back in Fort Campbell, Kentucky, but in a much less luxurious setting. In fact, the tent was quite basic at best. As with my first summons, I made sure to be prompt with my arrival. The major started the conversation.

"Miller, how would you like to go back to the States?"

Not knowing where he was going, I replied, "Yes, sir. But may I ask why?"

"Okay," he said. "Here's the deal. You don't have enough enlistment time, so you must re-up for four more years. Is that a problem?"

Confused, I said, "Well, sir. What is the offer?"

"Oh. Did you not receive papers from headquarters informing you that you have been selected to go to OCS back in Fort Benning, Georgia?"

"No, sir. I didn't."

"Well, is re-enlistment a problem, Miller?"

"Yes, sir. That would interfere with my goals."

I could sense his agitation and his inability to comprehend why I would have to think about such a generous offer. It was, indeed, an honor to be considered for OCS, but an additional four-year commitment was not even a consideration for me. Next, came a barrage of questions: "Exactly what are your goals, Miller?"

"Sir, my family back in Arkansas was poorer than church-house mice, but I really wanted to go to college."

"If you intended to go to college, why did you join the Army?"

"Because I was told that when I completed my obligation to the U.S. Army, my college expenses would be partially covered."

"Do you not like the Airborne, Miller?"

"I truly do like it, Sir."

The major made no effort to conceal his indignation. "Miller, this is a tremendous opportunity for you—a country boy from Arkansas who has trouble keeping his stripes on his sleeves. Explain to me why your rank goes up and down like a window shade."

I knew I needed to tread lightly. I cautiously replied, "The truth is, Sir, I come from a poor part of Arkansas where fist-fighting was a necessary way of life, and that has been a hard habit to break."

"I see here in your file where you struck a sergeant first class and received an Article 15. Is that correct?"

"Yes, Sir."

"Don't you realize striking a superior can result in a court-martial? The officers who recommended you for OCS had to overlook your Article 15. That doesn't happen every day, Miller."

My thoughts were running around in my head like a bunch of monkeys in a coconut tree. I could not commit to another four years in the military. The awkward silence was nerve-racking, but the major had not asked a question, so I knew not to speak. There was nothing more I could say to make the situation better, so my best option was to remain silent until the major spoke. Finally, he harshly said, "You're dismissed, Miller."

I quickly made my exit and ever so gently closed the tent flap. I heard my military file being slammed hard on the major's desk. I just kept going.

Our unit had settled in and developed a rather comfortable routine while stationed in Camp Wood, Kyushu, Japan. Five days a week, we started our day off early in the morning with a run, then exercise followed by breakfast. After breakfast, our specialty training continued.

One ordinary morning in early 1954, Mr. Classified was about to punch us in the face. At about

10:00 a.m., we were alerted that Rogue Group was to immediately assemble in the mess hall. After the head count was taken, our commander informed us that at 1:00 p.m. we were to reassemble in full combat gear including weapons, grenades, helmets, etc. Now, that got our attention. We were the most highly trained group in the Far East and were a little cocky about it. We were eager to put our skills to the test.

At 1:00 p.m. sharp, Rogue Group loaded onto two-and-a-half-ton trucks bound for the airport. We didn't waste any time boarding the plane and getting in the air. Only the officers and top non-commissioned officers (NCO's) were privy to the nature of our mission. At first, we paratroopers joked around with each other thinking this was just another training exercise.

My mind began to wander, and I thought about a rumor I had heard not long after graduating from jump school of a secret mission in Guatemala in Central America. Another group of forty or so highly trained paratroopers were loaded into a C-123 and flown to Guatemala to disband a military group that was the fighting arm of the Communist. When the paratroopers landed, they were "ready for bear," but the Communist brigade had vanished into the brush never to be found by the U.S. Bad Boys.

After an hour and a half into the flight, some of the soldiers, including me, began to doze off. By this time, we were all a little bit sleepy and a little bit frightened. Soon the plane began to lower its altitude signaling to us that we were about to land rather than jump. Relief replaced fear at that point. We were informed that this was a refueling stop on the island of Guam. We were given permission to go to the military post exchange (PX) and were told to be back on the plane in one hour. We purchased sweets and soda pops and exercised our eyes on the cute, curvy cashier.

An hour later, everyone was aboard the plane except for Sergeant First Class Lopes who was one of the best-liked sergeants in our group. The pilot waited about fifteen minutes for the sergeant who never returned. Finally, the pilot revved the engines, and we were once again airborne.

We made two more refueling stops—one on Okinawa and the last in Luzon in the Philippines. By the time we made the third stop, everyone was dog tired. However, we once again boarded that C-123 and headed off for a destination still unknown to us. We speculated that perhaps the plane had made a ~~1800~~ 180° turn while we were sleeping and that we were headed back to Camp Wood. No such luck!

A couple of hours before daybreak, a voice came over the intercom with a command: "Stand up and check your equipment." This actually meant to stand and check your partner's gear because it was easier to see the equipment of the man standing in front of you than to see your own.

The next order was, "Hook up and shuffle to the door."

Well, glory be! At this point, we all knew this was not a training exercise and fear gripped each of us. We were very familiar with the routine because of the numerous times we had practiced for this moment in training. It was a little different knowing that this was the real deal.

Next the red light popped on and we heard, "Stand in the door."

Then, the green light lit up, and we heard the loud and clear command, "Go."

Although it was pitch dark and we were all scared as Old Billy Heck, we went! Once on the ground, we gathered our 'chutes and assembled in a lighted area where, for the first time, we lesser lights were schooled on our highly classified mission. Our assignment was to make our way through Cambodia into Viet Nam, destroying any Viet Nam troops we encountered.

As Rogue Group stood there frozen with a combination of fear and excitement, one braver trooper sounded off rather loudly. "Sir, where are we?" A roar of laughter was spontaneous.

The captain in charge politely responded. "At the present time, we are standing on the end of the secondary runway of Don Mueang Air Strip in Bangkok, Thailand. This is where we jumped earlier this morning."

Within two days, we were in Viet Nam but found it difficult to make contact with the enemy. Our goal was to scare the North Vietnamese into abandoning their aggression. Scare the North Vietnamese? Well, as history tells us, they don't scare easily. We did not know that while we bad boys were doing our thing in Viet Nam, the U.S. Marines were conducting an amphibious mission nearby. We learned years later that our presence caused the Viet Cong to scamper into underground tunnels like roaches in a dark kitchen when a light comes on.

On a much larger scale, unknown to the Rogue Group at the time, the French (not the United States) were engaged in fighting the Viet Cong and North Vietnamese. It was several years later before President Eisenhower first sent a few unarmed observers into Viet Nam. Bad idea. They were picked off like sitting ducks. During the next two presidencies—Kennedy's and Johnson's—American troops were sent by the hundreds of thousands into Viet Nam. Finally, in 1973, President Nixon, against strong opposition, sent American troops into Cambodia to destroy munitions including all fighting arms stored by the North Vietnamese. This bold action finally brought that dreadful war to an end. Our secret mission of 1954 was years before the United States became overtly involved in that conflict.

Following our return to Camp Wood after our covert mission, we all became concerned about Sgt. Lopes whom we all held in high regard. He hadn't shown up in five days. We were worried that he might be classified as a deserter rather than absent without leave (AWOL). Captain Lavendar became very protective of Sgt. Lopes. It was certain, we thought, that Lopes would be demoted in rank from sergeant first class to private which would lead to his transfer to another unit. Well, lo and behold, on the sixth day, he showed up. We lower-ranking troopers never learned what went on. We waited and waited for his stripes to be taken away. That never happened. Obviously, his extended absence was somehow never reported to higher authorities otherwise he would have undoubtedly been severely punished.

Many years later, probably forty or so, I paid Sgt. Lopes a surprise visit at his home in Clarksville, Tennessee. He answered my knock on his door gave me a very cool reception—even after I told him my name. He denied ever knowing me or serving in the 508th Regimental Combat Team. Sgt. Nathan Griffith told me that he, too, once paid a visit to Lopes and received the same icy treatment. What a mystery!

Soon after returning stateside, I decided to get a furlough and return home for a visit. Only the Good

Lord knows why I thought it would be a good idea to hitchhike to my home in Arkansas. To begin my journey, I asked one of my buddies, Towny Mosely, to drive me out of our base to the highway that went straight to Memphis, across the Mississippi River, and into Arkansas.

Luck was on my side, and I only had to change cars two times before I got to downtown Memphis. The nice guy who drove me into Memphis had to let me out in a terrible part of town because that was where the exit he needed to take happened to be. I was quite-a-bit nervous, but Jesus was looking out for this little paratrooper. I had only been standing next to my old duffle bag for about twenty minutes when a fellow and his lovely wife rolled up next to me. The gentleman rolled down his window and asked where I was headed. I told him my destination was south of Little Rock.

The kind driver said, "We're headed for Oklahoma. If you and that bag can get in the back seat, I can take you to Little Rock." As we traveled together, we had an extremely pleasant two-hour visit. I learned that the man was a career navy guy with fourteen years of service under his belt.

I was dropped off in North Little Rock in an area that was familiar to me. I had spent part of a summer with Uncle Dois and Aunt Bonnie who once lived in the exact neighborhood where I was dropped off. I soon found myself on Roosevelt Avenue in Little Rock. This location was the beginning of the highway out of Little Rock that would start my fifty-mile journey home.

A mist of rain started to fall, so I found shelter under a large, metal Esso sign. However, the sign cast a shadow that left me standing in the dark—not a good situation for a hitchhiker who needed to be seen. My only options were to stand in the darkness with the sign protecting me from the elements or to stand in the rain. I could not afford to get wet not knowing what was ahead of me that night.

I had been standing in the shadows for about thirty minutes knowing that it was difficult for drivers to see me. It must have been 8:00 p.m. or later. I was becoming concerned. Suddenly a car from the opposite direction began to slow down and came to a stop right across from me. I tried to see who was driving thinking it might be a policeman who was going to tell me to move on. I could not tell the make of the car.

As unbelievable as it might sound, a familiar voice called out, "Johnny, hold on. I'll turn around and be right back." The driver didn't have to identify himself. I knew immediately it was my cousin, Shorty Ballard. There was no one else with a voice like his.

My first cousin, Shorty, was a well-built, friendly guy that everyone seemed to like. Shorty's mother and my father were siblings. As a kid, I never knew that his real name was Balus O'Neal Ballard. Shorty was physically stronger than all of us fellows in his age range. He and I were reared only four or five miles apart but seldom saw one another except for family reunions. As years went by, I became closer to one of his younger brothers, Colen, whom everyone called Butch.

Shorty, who was a good academic student, dropped out of school in eleventh grade and subsequently joined the U.S. Navy. Tragically, Shorty had only served in the Navy a little over a year when his father, Fenter Ballard, was killed in a mining accident. Shorty was immediately discharged to return home and help his mother care for his five younger siblings.

Our lives took us in different directions. Several years passed before I saw Shorty again. Who would have ever guessed that when I found myself stranded and alone in a large city on a dark and rainy night, that our paths would cross again for the first time in years? My cousin appeared at a time when I desperately needed help.

Shorty drove me all the way home. He introduced me to his date, Rosie Jean. They and another couple were headed to Jacksonville to watch a drive-in movie, but Shorty didn't think twice about picking me up and driving fifty miles in the opposite direction to deliver me to my front door. I tried, without success, to get him to tell me how, on God's green Earth, he recognized me in the dark shadows from across two lanes of traffic. What a miracle! I teared up. Shorty later told me that the four of them resumed their double date after dropping me off and were able to catch a late drive-in movie up in Jacksonville.

Shorty soon married Rosie Jean. They spent many happy years together before his death in 1997. Rosie Jean passed away in 2023. Shorty's brother, Butch, lives in Bryant, Arkansas. He is a huge fan of Corvettes. Shorty's other siblings—Kay, Larry, and Jerry—all live in our hometown of Poyen, Arkansas.

I mentioned earlier that it was four decades after I was discharged from the U.S. Army before I saw Sgt. Lamirande and Capt. Lavendar again. That reunion took place after my wife and I had both retired and were living in Little Rock, Arkansas. Out of the blue, I received a circular in the mail from Sgt. Garland Wright inviting my wife and me to attend a military get-together at his ranch. I recognized the sergeant's name and remembered that I had served with him in the 101st. I had not known him well while enlisted, but I learned that after he left the military, Sgt. Wright went to work serving barbecue sandwiches for a chain that he later bought. That savvy business venture made him a very wealthy man. I wasn't sure why I was receiving the invitation from him until I flipped it over.

On the back of the circular was a hand-written message: "The Captain and Sgt. Lamirande have especially requested your presence in Clarksville, Tennessee, on these dates."

Emma and I accepted the invitation. We stayed in a large Holiday Inn in Clarksville. After checking in, I went down to the hotel lobby to wait for Sgt. Lamirande to arrive. It seems he was already there and had appointed someone to keep watch and let him know when I arrived. When I entered the lobby, someone shouted, "He's here."

Just then, the back door of the lobby opened. What happened next was totally unexpected. Sgt. Nathaniel Lamirande burst into the room and broke into a sprint straight toward me, passing through a dining area and large lobby. My big ol' rough, tough sergeant grabbed me up and gave me the biggest bear hug I had ever had. It was a little painful, if I'm honest.

Sgt. Lamirande gently planted me just a foot or so in front of him and said, "Let me look at you." If that doesn't bring tears to your eyes, then you're all dried up.

As we spent hours reminiscing and catching up on four decades of life, my sergeant instantly hit it off with Emma in the same way he and I had bonded all those years ago. What a wonderful reunion we all shared! Sadly, Sgt. Lamirande died shortly after that wonderful gathering. Man, I sure did love that old sucker.

When Emma and I arrived at the Wright ranch, the captain, his wife, and his younger daughter, Paula, were already there. The bond the captain and I shared forty years earlier was still just as strong when we reunited. The women in our lives immediately connected. The captain, his wife, and Paula wanted to explore the town with us. Although I had been the captain's driver during our time together in the military, he insisted on doing the driving that day. Period. This humble action was his way of showing me the utmost respect. The unspoken message was one of equality. For several years after that initial reunion, Emma and I annually met the captain, his wife, and Paula in Clarksville, Tennessee, which just happened to be equal distances from our homes in Arkansas and Georgia respectively. What wonderful times we shared!

Near-death Experience at Francois Creek

To my grandchildren: This story about your Papaw might very well fall into the category of "truth that is stranger than fiction." Back in 1957, ol' John Buck Miller was a different person from the man you know today as Papaw. He was a rough-cut redneck toughie whose favorite pastimes were hunting, fishing, and even scrapping a bit here and there if necessary. Your mothers (Leticia and Michelle) have no recollection of that young man, but Jugi could tell you more about who that scoundrel was before she and God co-conspired to refine him. You owe them both a debt of gratitude. Without Jugi's unconditional love and God's amazing grace, ol' John Buck might not have survived to tell this story. I am, without a doubt, a better man because of their influences. This story is one example of how one little plot twist could have resulted in a very different and tragic end. Had Death won the Battle of Francois (pronounced Frans-way) Creek, your Papaw, who was a twenty-two year old newlywed, would have never had children and would have left no descendants—meaning you, my beloved grandchildren, would have never experienced life.

The most harrowing experience of my life, to date, took place on a frigid December day in 1957 in Grant County, Arkansas. Temperatures that day hovered in the low twenties. As a youngster, I spent countless days wandering and exploring the deep woods of the Saline River area just east of our log house. After being gone from my home and serving in the military for more than three years, my first trip back as a married man was one that I had eagerly anticipated for some time. I could hardly bridle my excitement as I prepared to revisit the familiar fishing and hunting grounds that held so many of my most treasured childhood memories. This day (like most any day I woke up in Poyen, Arkansas) was one that I thought would be perfect for trudging through the stomping grounds of my youth.

I set out for the day's adventure with only my shotgun, hunting coat, cap, and gloves as companions. I wanted no distractions as I spent a few private hours with the land and elements of nature that had been my haven for so many years. As it turned out, choosing not to take a buddy, or even my faithful dog, Hunter, was a calculated decision that likely contributed to my survival of the day's adventure. I do, however, regret that there was not another person along to witness and chronicle the horrifying events of that fateful day. I fear that telling the story myself in the honest context it deserves may sound boastful. Be assured that there is not one ounce of vainglory in my heart. Humility and gratitude to God Almighty fill my soul when I reflect on the role He surely played in guiding me that day. Now, more than six decades later, the particulars of that experience are so deeply and vividly etched in my memory, I am confident that every detail is recounted with one hundred percent accuracy. Those recollections are as fresh and emotionally charged as if they happened yesterday and still trigger goose bumps all over my body. I have only shared the highlights of the Francois Creek experience with a few select people who are closest to me, but no one (except my sweet bride, Emma) has heard all the details until now.

    Freshly out of the paratroopers, I was more physically and mentally fit than I had ever been—attributes that may have given me a sense of invincibility. I recall that I hurriedly finished breakfast that morning and commenced with preparations for my long-anticipated trek to the Saline River bottoms. As I cleaned and oiled my old twelve-gauge shotgun, I began visualizing and mentally mapping out the day's journey. I could walk about four miles an hour, so it would take me about two hours to reach the river, factoring in the time it takes to cross Francois Creek. I began to envision the deep woods that were beckoning me. Although bitterly cold, the weather had been dry in our area for some time as evidenced by firm, dry ground and the crunch of brittle leaves when tromping through wooded areas. My first hurdle, a little more than a mile into my expedition, would be crossing Francois Creek—a large body of flowing water. I recalled that I usually crossed the creek at a spot known to locals as the "School House Ford"—a shallow place in the creek that usually allowed one to wade safely to the other side. Regardless of where I chose to cross, reaching the Saline River from the west side of the creek would require traveling another distance of more than two miles.

The forest welcomed me with familiar sights, sounds, and aromas that initiated a boxcar full of nostalgia. The overcast day with low-hanging clouds generated within me a sense of being totally alone—not lonely at all—but a peaceful and serene oneness with my surroundings. The calm was a balm for my soul, just as I had anticipated it would be. I was very aware that even skilled, experienced hunters and explorers often lost their bearings on overcast days such as this with the sun eliminated as a reference for direction. It occurred to me that outdoorsmen rely on landmarks and terrain as their guides in the same way city dwellers depend on street signs and road maps. I reminded myself that I was very familiar with the land that I had hunted and fished since the time I was knee-high to a bull frog. I was certain I could navigate my way through those woods with my eyes closed if need be.

As I approached Francois Creek, an enormous oak tree that had been uprooted demanded my attention. The Goliath of a tree had likely been brought down by a combination of erosion of the creek bank and strong winds. The giant had fallen in such a way that it came to rest with its sprawling roots—now washed clean of the dirt that had once bound it to the ground—on one side of the creek and the limbs that formed its crest on the opposite bank. Its massive trunk, still solid and strong, spanned the breadth of the creek at one of the deepest parts, creating an ideal foot log. What an unexpected delight! I easily strode across the large tree trunk and reached the opposite bank quickly. With Francois Creek behind me, I still had more than two miles to go before I reached the river. I was confident that my knowledge of the woods and its landmarks would keep me oriented; however, as the day wore on and I neared the Saline River, I began to get an eerie sense that it was time to head back home—an inkling that danger loomed nearby. Years of experience in this woodland had taught me to trust my instincts.

At that exact moment, a deafening roaring sound like nothing I had ever heard before seemed to envelop me. I was suddenly seized with intense fear—something I had never experienced in the woods that had always been my fortress. I struggled to mentally identify the thunderous noise. In another setting, I might have thought it to be a squadron of airplanes flying low overhead or perhaps several trains converging from every direction.

    I soon became keenly aware that the roaring sound was that of a vast amount of murky water suddenly forcefully flooding into the area and surging over the dry leaves that carpeted the forest floor surrounding me. The swift, frigid ambush of water was rapidly inundating my surroundings and seemed to be coming from every direction. Almost instantly, muddy water covered my boots. I instinctively grabbed a small tree and held on for dear life to avoid being swept off my feet. I was soon encased by ankle-deep water that was rising rapidly. Ice began to form on my clothes that had not yet been submerged but had become soaking wet from the spray and mist created by the raging water violently crashing into everything in its path. Suddenly, the peace I had relished shortly before morphed into terror. I became incredibly aware that I was totally alone with the angry forces of nature that had, at this point, waged war against me and become my enemy.

    I later learned that areas just slightly north of my childhood home, including the river bottoms, had been getting steady bouts of rain for several days prior to my day of hunting. The steady, daily precipitation had created saturated ground in those areas. Just the night before, a torrential downpour had caused area creeks, streams, and rivers to overflow their banks. Because of that combination of forces of nature, I now found myself surrounded by a muddy sea of ever-rising floodwater that was vigorously making its way southward.

At that time in my life, I considered myself to be fearless. I would have taken on Satan himself with confidence that he would have been overmatched! But at that moment, ol' John Buck was petrified. Recognizing my need to think quickly and clearly, I began to rein in the assault of emotions that were running unrestrained through my body and mind like a bunch of hyperactive spider monkeys playfully scurrying through the mangrove canopy of a tropical rain forest. I had to get myself together.

With approximately two hours of daylight left and miles between me and Francois Creek, I had no more time to indulge in the paralyzing fear and panic to which I had momentarily succumbed. My only thoughts were of living to see another day and reuniting with my beautiful wife—and doing so on dry land. I began harnessing the survival skills I had acquired during my training to become a U.S. Paratrooper and Army Ranger. However, the challenges I faced for the next two or three hours were far more dangerous than any I had ever experienced. This was no training mission. This was do or die. Certainly, my military training and conditioning had prepared me, as much as possible, for the physical and mental challenges I now faced. My physical strength and mental acuity would be tested in ways that would take them to their outermost limits. Although I was well-trained and prepared for war, I never imagined that I would find myself squared off against the horrifying forces of Mother Nature. I do not recall consciously consulting with the Big Guy upstairs or asking Him for help, but I am now certain that He extended immeasurable mercy and grace to ol' John Buck that day. I was toe-to-toe and nose-to-nose with Death more than once that afternoon. Undoubtedly, it was God's guidance and intervention that ultimately brought about my deliverance from my own impaired decision-making abilities.

Still clinging to the tree I had grabbed hold of to remain upright, I began to quickly take inventory and assess my situation. It seemed I had two options: climb a tree and wait for the rising waters to recede or somehow maneuver myself through that angry, raging sea and make my way back home. My sense of reason immediately began to discount the former for a host of reasons. I was already wet and cold. My clothes were literally freezing on my body. Hypothermia would surely soon begin to set in. With no way of knowing how long it would take for the floodwaters to recede, the first option was quickly losing its appeal.

Then a thought came to me that discounted that option altogether: "What if one of my friends or family members came to search for me and lost his life in the process?" Suddenly, option one became an abandoned consideration. My only alternative was to push my wiry, physically fit body to its limit. Not to boast, but at that time in my life, I was not fazed when confronted with strong opposition. I didn't go looking for trouble, but if it came knocking, I didn't back down from it, either. If you had to go to battle, ol' John Buck was one you would want to take with you. Now was the time for me to harness every resource available and get myself out of this life-threatening situation.

I became acutely aware that in addition to the sun being taken out of the equation for ascertaining direction, clues from the terrain were now being removed as the rising water quickly camouflaged landmarks that had served as my guides. Ditches, sloughs, gullies, stump holes, fallen trees—literally every cue that this land had given me for most of my life was now obscured from view by shadowy floodwaters that made the entire woods appear to be of the same elevation lacking any identifiable features. I further observed that the water that had initially seemed to converge on me from all directions was moving briskly in one clear path. Finally, a directional clue. Hallelujah!

I knew immediately that the water was moving due south.

Because I had been traveling east toward the river, I deduced that I needed to travel south a good distance and then turn westward to get to the School House Ford, cross Francois Creek, and ultimately (if body and mind didn't fail me), return home to my sweet Emma. But how far south? How would I know when to turn west? What towering clue or landmark might be visible in the ever-rising water that was now creeping up my calves? My mind raced frantically as if hastily searching through manilla folders in a file cabinet for that one piece of pertinent information.

In a flash, I thought about John Pierce's field that had long since ceased being used for raising corn and was now overgrown with gum saplings and underbrush. I recalled that, for the most part, the barbed wire fence that marked the perimeters of the Pierce field was still intact except for a few short spans where neglected fence posts had either rotted down or given way to the force of falling limbs. The rusty, brittle barbed wire often snapped in two when severed boughs fell on it. My best and only plan was to move southward with the flow of the rushing water in hopes of finding that old, dilapidated property-line fence. If fortune was on my side and I didn't miss the Pierce field by passing through a downed section of the fence, I would then make a ninety-degree turn to my right which would put me traveling west. The very thought of getting my bearings and knowing with certainty that I was homeward bound energized me tremendously--revitalizing my freezing body and exhausted mind.

With my spirits lifted, the water didn't seem quite as cold and my steps not nearly as labored. Although the muddy sea that had become my constant companion had only reached knee level, I was soaked to my armpits due to my feet sliding into ruts and ditches that caused me to dip deeper into the muddy water. Floating debris—including leaves, twigs, and slabs of tree bark—picked up pace as it drifted downstream, communicating to me that the floodwater was continuing to rise. Objects moving on the water's surface are sure signs of rising water. Better news would have been for the floating trash to begin to collect and form drifts which would have indicated that the water was receding.

My perilous trek soon took a promising turn. Much to my delight, I ran smackdab into John Pierce's fence. To make the encounter even sweeter, just a few feet away stood Mr. Pierce's oversized homemade wooden gate—still tilted just the way it had been for as long as I could remember. The wooden structure was about half submerged, swaying back and forth to the rhythm of the flowing water. For a brief moment, joy flooded my soul as I found myself basking in sweet memories of people and landmarks that were so beautifully woven into the tapestry of my life. I randomly calculated that my chances of finding that fence under such duress were no more than twenty percent without God's help, leaving an eighty percent probability of the opposite outcome. How could anyone doubt that God was with ol' John Buck?

My temporary reprieve suddenly came to an abrupt halt when I stepped into a waist-deep hole obscured from my view by my enemy—the muddy sea that still encompassed me. This was the first of a series of baptisms I endured that afternoon and one that caused me to be momentarily disoriented. However, I quickly regained my composure and my footing. I sloshed my way back to the gate where I firmly planted my backside against the structure so that I was facing due west. With uplifted spirits and renewed grit, I began trudging homeward.

What happened next is nothing short of miraculous. If finding the Pierce gate was the equivalent of finding a nugget of gold, my next discovery was like tapping into the motherlode. As I constantly scanned the horizon, tree line, and sky searching for signs to point me toward home, I discovered an opening in the tree line that was as familiar as if the image had been captured in an old, cherished photograph. Instantly, I became aware that the slightly higher and smoother ground I was walking on beneath the floodwaters was the middle of an old wagon trail that meandered westward and that would lead me directly to the School House Ford. All I had to do was keep looking up and allow the tree line to direct my path. The symbolism of looking upward for guidance was confirmation enough for me that this good fortune was a gift straight out of Heaven.

Finding the Pierce field and gate and then discovering the wagon trail surely boosted my morale, but my mental and physical capabilities were gradually deteriorating, succumbing to the toll of combatting the elements with no way of knowing when the next step might literally take me under. The tree line that had been my guide was, at times, hard to follow. Decades-old oak trees grew on both sides of the trail. In places, their outstretched and overlapping limbs obscured my view.

In desperation, a bit of knowledge that had been tucked away somewhere in my gray matter, unneeded for many years but now essential to my survival, suddenly emerged. I was reminded that many years ago, when this old wagon trail had been heavily traveled by loggers, the often-overloaded wagons bound for the sawmill in Poyen frequently hauled logs that extended beyond the shoulders of the road and scraped the bark off the trees that lined each side of the wagon trail. At that moment, I was so thankful that my brain, now sluggish from the day's brutality and extreme cold, was somehow able to retrieve that dormant bit of knowledge. Those old scrapes were pointing me toward home as if they were flashing neon arrows. I later marveled that those decades-old scars on those trees helped pilot me home. What a gift!

More than a few times, I either slid off the shoulder of the trail or stepped into a hole that caused me to become totally submerged. The first full-body immersion at the Pierce field gate took me by surprise and required a moment to mentally recuperate. Subsequent plunges became expected and were only fleeting annoyances. But I was growing weary. I felt that I was at the end of my rope with the knot slipping. I didn't know how much longer my body could withstand the elements, and I was conscious of the dullness that was gradually overtaking my mind. The waist-deep water was still steadily rising. I thought about the foot log that had afforded me safe passage across Francois Creek earlier in the day and knew that it would now be completely underwater thought that only contributed to the desperation that was beginning to overwhelm me.

Just then, muffled by the continuous drone of the raging floodwaters, I heard a familiar sound. As I focused my attention on the sound, I realized that what

I was hearing was quacking ducks. I could tell by the cadence of their chorus that they were feeding. I remembered a large knoll just east of Francois Creek and about a hundred yards north of the ford, well-known to all who hunted the area as home to a duck roost. That meant that I was within a very short distance—no more than a few yards—of the creek bank. Hallelujah! I regained motivation to press on because I knew that my feathered friends were either enjoying a feast of acorns on elevated land or were in still waters.

My next thought was quite sobering. Because I had been unaware of my exact location, I could have easily stumbled into the now raging Francois Creek. The depth and swiftness of the violent torrent would have swept me off my feet, and I would not have been able to regain my footing given my weakened condition. I would have most assuredly drowned. Once again, I found myself immensely thankful that I was by myself. Had I brought along a hunting buddy or even my dog, chances are I would have drowned long before reaching this point. I absolutely would not have let either of them perish if I had breath and an iota of strength within me. Getting only myself this far was almost beyond my ability. I suspect that if I had brought companions, we would have all met our maker that day in the flooded Saline River bottoms.

With Francois Creek within spittin' distance I, once again, had rekindled hope, strength, and energy. A quick inventory of the debris floating downstream revealed a stout stick about five feet long—just the proper length for poking and probing the ground in front of me to help avoid inadvertently stepping into the creek. As I searched for the creek bank without the benefit of being able to see the ground I was walking on, I thought about how blind people use their white-tipped canes to scan their surroundings for obstacles or orientation markers. In that moment, I could relate to their challenges.

I became aware that the water level that had been above my waist seconds ago was now below my knees, yet the swiftness remained the same. That could only mean that I was standing at the very edge of the creek. The land, for several feet near the bank of a stream, creek, or river generally becomes higher—a phenomenon of nature known as sedimentation which is caused by the process of sediment (in this case, dirt) being deposited along the edge of the body of water when flooding occurs.

Crossing Francois Creek for the second time that day was, by far, the most difficult and terrifying hurdle of the whole ordeal—quite a contrast to the quick and easy passage the massive foot log had allowed me a few hours earlier. The water ahead of me was flowing faster than the water behind me—positive affirmation that Francois Creek was directly in front of me. The creek was now violently raging. My body had become almost numb from constant exposure to the frigid water, yet I knew I had to somehow get to the opposite bank. Chills ran up and down my spine at the thought of plunging into the swift water. From the recesses of my memory, a story emerged of waters parting and weary travelers pursued by their enemy walking across on dry land. I would have loved nothing more than for that to be the "and he lived happily ever after" ending to my story. My tale, like the one of ol' Moses, may sound fictitious; however, both stories are absolutely true.

    Refocusing on the task at hand, I extended my crude stick a couple of feet in front of me and gingerly stabbed at the short span of elevated ground that lay between me and Francois Creek. The discovery that there was no solid surface to be found only inches away sobered me. I instinctively took a couple of steps backward to avoid being swept into the turbulent body of water taunting me. I knew what I had to do. In preparation for the plunge awaiting me, I removed my old twelve-gauge. I then removed my half-frozen hunting coat. I knew that, because of their weight, my coat and gun may have to be sacrificed to the enemy as my cap and gloves had been much earlier in this war. Cradling my coat and gun under my left arm, I probed the ground in front of me with my stick once more until I was within inches of the creek bank. It was now or never.

I harnessed every scintilla of physical and mental strength within me and plunged myself into the violent stream with my right arms and legs fighting franticly with physical strength I did not know I possessed. To my amazement, the rushing water seemed to lift me upward and thrust me toward the west bank as if a rope were tied around my waist, suspended from a tree on the opposite shore, and propelling me forward. This is in stark contrast to the typical behavior of swift water which is to force one under.

I was across the raging creek in seconds. I grabbed hold of a small tree that was firmly rooted in the west bank. My feet quickly found the slippery wall of the embankment. As I was pulling and clawing my way to the top, I suddenly felt a tug on my coat. I jerked as forcefully as I could and freed it. Physically exhausted and mentally spent, I somehow managed to reach the slick west bank of Francois Creek. Glory hallelujah! When I stood up, I was in waist-deep water and too depleted of energy and cognitive ability to rejoice or celebrate. The increasing effect of hypothermia was quickly diminishing my capacity to function and to make rational decisions as is clearly demonstrated by my next move.

As I took inventory and prepared for the last lag of my quest, I discovered that my shotgun was missing. Without weighing the consequences, I hurriedly hung my old, soaked hunting coat on a tree limb and headed back toward Francois Creek to retrieve my gun. I methodically traced my steps back toward that little tree rooted in the west bank—the one that had aided me in climbing out of the creek bed just moments before. My only thought was of freeing my twelve-gauge from the clutches of the enemy and reclaiming it as my own. I quickly located and grabbed the little tree and slithered back into the murky and swift creek. When my boots touched the lower part of the bank wall, I felt my gun. It was firmly restrained near the bed of the creek. Using roots that were embedded in the wall of the creek bank, I maneuvered myself under the water and forcefully snatched my gun from the mangled nest of limbs and debris that held it hostage. I then used those same roots to propel myself upward and back to that sweet little tree. Soon I was once again standing on the west bank of Francois Creek—this time with my old scatter-load in tow.

  I continued my journey home following the old dirt trail west of Francois Creek that was as familiar to me as the chug holes in the lane to Grandmaw's house. I managed to maneuver myself back into my hunting coat which offered no warmth at this point but was easier to wear than to carry. I waded and sloshed through a shallow slough that brought me to higher ground. I was amazed that such a short distance could separate land that was disastrously flooded from land that was bone dry.

I trudged homeward on that old, familiar dirt road that would eventually lead past Howell Webb's place—about a mile from my home—and then on to the main highway that would take me to my front door. I was aware that I was more than slightly dazed and that my movements had become somewhat robotic, but I somehow managed to keep putting one foot in front of the other. As the Webbs' house came into view, I saw a clean, shiny car backing out of the driveway. I could see that Lyndell, Mr. Webb's son, was the driver.

Lyndell saw me and immediately drove up beside me—behavior consistent with folks who lived in that area. Granted, chances were good that Lyndall would encounter a familiar face, but his compassion and kindness would have been extended with equal zeal to a total stranger. That was just the standard for country folks in that part of the world. With the engine of his car still running, Lyndell quickly got out and came to my aide. He insisted that I get into his car, ignoring my objections that my wet, muddy clothes and boots would soil his immaculate vehicle. I was in no condition to debate, so I did my best to respectfully follow his instructions. He quickly removed my gun from my frozen grip and placed it in his car. He then literally picked me up and deposited me into the back seat. My violent shivering caused his car to shake. Lyndell delivered me home to Emma and made sure that I and my shotgun made it safely inside.

In the safety and comfort of my warm, dry home my body began to thaw. I recall feeling intense physical pain for the first time that day. Oh, I had been miserably cold and horrifically uncomfortable, but this was the first actual pain I had experienced. During the next four or five hours, my body temperature slowly returned to normal. Miraculously, I recovered fully within a few hours and did not so much as have a sniffle from all the extreme exposure.

It will forever remain a mystery as to whether I would have been able to travel that last mile home without help. For Lyndell's kind rescue, I remain eternally grateful and told him so many times. Both he and his father, Mr. Webb, have long-since gone to be with Jesus. The old dirt road that led me to their homeplace has faded and become overgrown with trees. Although Francois Creek and the Saline River continue to flow toward the Mississippi and on down to New Orleans, undoubtedly still providing a refuge for avid outdoorsmen, I no longer spend time there having lost my desire to pursue wild game many years ago.

Nevertheless, I still possess that old twelve-gauge shotgun and hunting coat. I just cannot bring myself to part with either—the two companions who shared and survived the Francois Creek near-death experience with me.

    I am now eighty-nine years old and can say that my greatest accomplishment in my life thus far was not overcoming the enemy at Francois Creek, rather it was winning the heart of my sweet Emma. My mind often drifts back to that December day in 1957 when I came fearfully close to making her a young widow. How very thankful I am to have survived that terrifying flood and to have since been blessed to build a wonderful life and create a beautiful family with my bride of sixty-seven years! They say, "All's well that ends well." This is one of ol' John Buck's stories that ended well.

Grandpaw's Brother Becomes Murder Suspect

Grandpaw's stories never failed to amuse and entertain me, but one that he didn't share with me until I was in my teens still gives me the willies. I was not the first or only Johnny Miller in the family. You see, I was named after my Grandpaw's brother, Johnny. The story about my great-uncle evidently made quite a splash in and around the area where the Millers lived. Had the story made the newspaper, the headline might have read, *"Johnny Miller Suspected of Murdering his Wife for Another Woman."* I only hope that if such an article exists that any twenty-first century readers who know ol' John Buck will pay careful attention to the dates of the events and calculate that the murder suspect could not possibly be me. I was just a pup when the incident happened.

When Grandpaw deemed me mature enough to understand the saga of my namesake, he told me the story of a cool, cloudless Saturday morning around 1939 or 1940 when he set out to return a saddle horse, ol' Rex, he had borrowed several days earlier from his brother, Johnny. Grandpaw's horse had stepped into a gopher hole and was lame at the time. Johnny and his wife, Louise (who was an immigrant from Czechoslovakia), lived in a quiet, sleepy little place about two miles from a small settlement known as Traskwood. Grandpaw sometimes rode his horse to the rural settlement to buy goods at the General Store, stocking up with enough food and supplies to last a few weeks or with what his horse could carry. The store was owned and operated by Mr. Winters—a spindly, clean-shaven, white-haired old man who always gave the youngsters, and sometimes the ladies, a stick of peppermint candy.

Grandpaw was a kind old German gentleman. He was about five feet nine inches tall and weighed about one hundred seventy pounds. He was highly respected by all, including family members. In his younger days, he was a golden glove boxer in Nebraska. Grandpaw was more successful and had more money than any of his siblings including my great-uncle, Johnny.

During this time, there was an oil boom in southern Arkansas in and around the town of El Dorado. The boom attracted a lot of get-rich-quick speculators. Uncle Johnny formed a loose partnership with two men from Malvern—one was a lawyer, the other a doctor. The threesome invested their time, energy, and money into the oil boom in Union County, Arkansas. Well, as the old Arkansas saying goes, "They lost their britches."

Uncle Johnny had to tell the family about his oil dealings because he had "borrowed" his gambling money from his (and Grandpaw's) mother. The doctor, in turn, had borrowed quite a large sum of money from

Uncle Johnny. As is true of so many debtors, the gambling trio never repaid their debts, only made empty promises to do so. Information on the lawyer is scant, but each of these three wanna-be oil tycoons played a major role in Grandpaw's saga. Now, on with the story.

When Grandpaw arrived at his brother's house, he fed, watered, and brushed down ol' Rex before rattling the front door hoping to be greeted by his brother. When no one responded, Grandpaw went around to the side door and did the same. Again, no response. It was not uncommon in those days for folks to leave their doors unlocked, so Grandpaw gave the door a tug. It was unlocked, so in he went.

Now, Grandpaw was a man of principle and a tough ol' buzzard, but he confessed to me that from the moment he stepped foot into Johnny and Louise's house, he had an eerie feeling that caused goosebumps to pop up all over his body. Grandpaw made his way through the quiet but creaky house. As he cracked open the door to the back bedroom, he immediately saw Louise. She was lying face down atop a bed that had obviously not been slept in since being made up. Grandpaw called out to her. She did not respond. He crept closer and gently shook her hoping to awaken her; however, her body was stiff and cold. Grandpaw immediately knew that Louise was deceased, and had been for some time. Rigor mortis had already set in.

Grandpaw quickly left the bedroom, closed the door, and went outside to gather his thoughts.

He asked himself, "What should I do? Where is my brother?"

Because there were no phones in the house, there was no way for him to communicate with the outside world. He knew the law required that the discovery of a corpse be reported to local authorities; nevertheless, Grandpaw seriously considered resaddling ol' Rex and going back home as if he had never been there. With more questions than answers racing in his head, Grandpaw took a seat on a tree stump, lit up his pipe, and continued pondering what he should do, all the while hoping his brother would come driving up.

Uncle Johnny was one of the few people in that area who owned a vehicle—a 1927 Model T Ford. The car was not at home. Grandpaw considered that perhaps Johnny had gone somewhere and that his car had broken down. Since it was the weekend, a mechanic would be hard to find. Perhaps that would explain why Johnny had been away from home long enough for his wife to die and then for her lifeless body to lay on her bed and develop rigor mortis.

Grandpaw was a man who was attentive to details, a characteristic he shared with his brother. Still considering fleeing the scene, Grandpaw reasoned that if he did, Johnny would surely see ol' Rex's hoof prints in the loose dirt and know that he had been there which would create suspicion in Johnny's mind. Grandpaw decided his best course of action was to leave ol' Rex in the pasture, walk home, and do nothing until he was informed of Louise's demise. When and if the time came that he needed to talk about returning ol' Rex, his plan was to admit that he brought the horse back to his brother's home and to cautiously deny going into the house.

He vowed, "I will say nothing to Maud (Grandmaw) or anyone else about going into Johnny and Louise's house so that no one will have to lie except me." With that resolve, Grandpaw headed home.

Two days filled with heavy rains passed. Johnny had still not shown up to tell Grandpaw about Louise's death. Grandpaw's brain was working overtime. Finally, two Hot Spring County deputies arrived on Grandpaw's doorstep. They broke the news of Louise's death to Grandpaw and Grandmaw.

Grandmaw, who knew nothing about what Grandpaw had seen at Johnny's house, began to wail loudly which helped Grandpaw cover his well-kept secret. Grandmaw excused herself so that her sobbing did not interfere with the deputies' business with Grandpaw.

One of the deputies said, "Mr. Miller, you brother told us that you were at his house a couple of days ago when he was away. He said you were there to return a horse you had borrowed from him."

"That's right."

Grandpaw told me he was on his toes and intended to be careful not to volunteer any extra information. He told himself to just answer any questions law authorities asked as briefly and simply as possible. Then came the next question from the deputy. "Did you go inside your brother's house?"

"No. I don't go inside other people's homes unless I'm invited. Besides, I was in a hurry to get back home and fix my broken cultivator."

Grandpaw said he immediately realized he had broken his own rule. He had not been asked why he was in a hurry to get home, yet he offered up a quickly made-up detail about a broken cultivator.

Grandpaw was not the only one on his toes that day. The second deputy piped up. "I just happened to notice a broken-down cultivator as we drove up. It did not appear to be repaired."

Grandpaw was a quick thinker. "Well," he said, "The damage was worse than I thought when I first looked at it. Turns out, I'll have to get a mail-order replacement plowshare that will have to be shipped out of Memphis."

The deputies seemed satisfied with Grandpaw's alibi and didn't have any more questions for him—at least, not for the moment. They said their goodbyes and shook his hand.

One of them said, "Someone will be back to see you, I'm sure."

Back at Uncle Johnny's house, the deputies found two partially empty bags of arsenic—a poison that could be purchased just about anywhere farm supplies were sold. Farmers sprinkled the poison on freshly dug potatoes to protect them from insects and to help with the curing process. Arsenic was not absorbed by the potatoes and was easily washed off. However, if ingested by humans, the chemical element could be deadly poisonous. Death by arsenic poisoning is a very slow and extremely painful process. Without going into gruesome details, suffice to say the visible evidence of someone dying from arsenic poisoning is easy to identify, which is what caught the deputies' attention at Johnny and Louise's house.

Following the investigation into Aunt Louise's death, a young prosecutor wanted fiercely to prosecute Uncle Johnny for murder. However, small-town politics and personal friendships were too heavily stacked against him. Family members strongly suspected that Uncle Johnny got away with murdering Aunt Louise.

Uncle Johnny's alibi, as told to the high sheriff, was that he was "away" and that his car broke down. He claimed that he spent a whole day and night sleeping in his broken-down car. Family members believed that the truth was that he was gone for two nights or more and very likely stayed all that time with his girlfriend whom he quickly married after Aunt Louise's funeral.

Uncle Johnny also told the high sheriff that he and Aunt Louise slept in separate bedrooms. Family members who knew them well said that was not so. The family had questions that were never answered to their satisfaction: *Why was Uncle Johnny "away" when Aunt Louise died? Why did he not just divorce her? Why did he allow her body to lie unattended for at least two days—maybe more?*

A young doctor new to the area signed Aunt Louise's death certificate and recorded the cause of death as "poison—possible homicide." The same doctor who had "partnered" with Uncle Johnny on the oil venture and who owed him a lot of money somehow got access to the death certificate. He lined through "poison—possible homicide" and wrote above it "death by natural causes." That document was a focal point during the legal proceedings.

The family frequently questioned why the doctor suddenly no longer owed Uncle Johnny money. That debt being "resolved" meant that Johnny's mother was not likely to ever be repaid the money he "borrowed" from her. Some said that Uncle Johnny also suddenly no longer had his prize bull and his three high-bred saddle horses, including ol' Rex. One family member swore all those assets went to the other oil partner—the one who was a lawyer.

Soon after Aunt Louise was buried, Uncle Johnny broke all family ~~times~~ ties and never visited us again. He quickly married his girlfriend, sold his farm, and moved to Benton, a nearby small town. Lucky for Uncle Johnny, he was never charged with any crime. However, his family knows the truth, and Someone else knows as well.

Roadside Ruckuses

Summer nights in central Arkansas can be almost unbearably stifling, but one particular night was an exception. It was one of those nights when wide-open windows in our home allowed an occasional cool breeze to sift through the screens—a most welcome comfort for my little family of four since we had no air conditioning. Our baby, Michelle, had been sick and fussy throughout the day. Emma, who was a senior at Henderson State University, had spent the time she wasn't tending to our sick child studying for two important tests scheduled for the following day. She was a little under the weather herself, but our busy life did not allow time for parents to give in to sickness. By the end of the day, we were both exhausted and looking forward to settling in for a good night's sleep. Little did we know that nightfall was going to bring with it a chain of surprises.

During the early years of married life, Emma and I lived along Highway 7 in Bismarck, Arkansas, a small community where everybody knew everybody. Our home was not far off the narrow and curvy highway that linked the college town of Arkadelphia to Hot Springs. Most of the time, traffic was light to moderate on the scenic, rural highway that snaked through the Ouachita Mountains and ran about fifty feet in front of our house.

The first surprise of the evening was that my parents showed up unexpectedly for one of their rare overnight visits just as the evening was fading into nightfall. It seems Emma's mother had called my mother and told her that our baby was sick. Well, with about an hour or so of daylight left, my parents packed their duds and set out on the one-hour road trip to our house. They arrived right at dusk. Emma and I fixed my parents some sandwiches and visited with them for a couple of hours before turning in.

The second surprise of the evening was a happy one. Michelle's temperature had broken, and she was obviously feeling better. She went right to sleep. Her older sister and all the adults followed suit. Our home was dead silent except for the familiar intermittent sound of cars passing by on Highway 7. We were accustomed to the sound of light traffic, so it actually lulled us to sleep.

Next came one of the most tragic and heartbreaking surprises of my life. Suddenly in the dark silence of that cool summer night, our whole household was awakened by deafening sounds of screeching tires and a series of explosions right outside our open windows. It sounded like two trains transporting explosive materials had collided head on. I quickly rushed to make sure my wife and two daughters were okay, then went to check on Mom and Dad. I was relieved to find that all my loved ones were safe and unharmed. The middle-of-the-night disturbance had caused our electricity to go out, so I used a flashlight to make my way through the house. I quickly located and lit our two "coal oil" (kerosene) lamps.

About that time, I heard someone pounding on our front door. I recognized the familiar voice of one of my friends, Royce Sheets, who was frantically calling out my name. I was relieved that it was a voice I recognized and not that of a stranger out to harm my family. I rushed to see what my friend needed.

As soon as I opened the door, I saw flashes of light in my front yard and directly across the highway. Severed electric wires were suspended in the air and were swaying back and forth in my front yard. Every time those wires touched together, they created a flash in the pitch-dark summer night. The night had again gone silent except for the human sounds of Royce intently talking to me and the haunting sound of someone across the highway moaning painfully.

As I tried to make sense of the scene unfolding before my eyes, Royce was desperately trying to tell me what had happened. I had to calm him down before I could understand any part of what he was attempting to tell me. I was finally able to begin piecing together what was happening based on what I could see and what Royce was communicating.

I knew that he and O'Neal Cook rode together to and from their jobs at Reynolds Metal Company in Gum Springs which was about thirty-five miles south of my house. They were headed home after "swing shift," so they were traveling north on Highway 7. O'Neal was driving when, right in front of my house, a southbound drunk driver crossed the center line and crashed, head on, into his car. Both cars tumbled and rolled, knocking over an electric pole leaving some electric lines snapped and others suspended slightly above the ground. Royce said that at first, neither he nor O'Neal seemed to be hurt, so they both got out of the car. As they tried to make their way to the highway and then to my house, O'Neal stumbled into one of those suspended electric wires. That is when the most tragic thing happened. Both of his legs were severed just above his knees.

As I began to grasp the seriousness of the situation, my instinct was to run across the highway to help O'Neal who I could still hear groaning in agony. Royce, realizing what I was about to do, restrained me. He pointed out a second set of electric wires that was suspended just a couple of feet in front of my porch steps. Royce had somehow managed to maneuver his way around and through the deadly maze of wires to get to my front door. God's angels were surely with him and gave him unbelievable protection. The harsh reality of the dreadful situation was that it was far too dangerous for either of us to try to go back through the obstacle course of hot wires and cables. The only thing we could do was try to get help there as quickly as possible.

As terrible as the situation was, O'Neal's legs were severed in such a way that blood veins and arteries were seared, preventing him from bleeding out while waiting for help to arrive. That poor man had to lie on the ground for three hours as electric company workers cautiously and hastily labored to disconnect power and make it safe for the ambulance to get in and emergency medical staff to get to O'Neal. What a miracle that he survived the terrible accident! The driver of the other vehicle was pronounced dead at the scene.

I did not see O'Neal the night of the accident but visited him almost daily as he was treated in the Veteran's Hospital on Roosevelt Street in Little Rock for the next three months. I worked nearby, so visiting him was convenient. He remained jovial and high-spirited throughout his recovery. As far as I know, he never once complained. He lived another twenty-one years. His wife, Bernice, told me later that I was his most loyal friend.

All these years later, I am still haunted by the sights and sounds of that cool, Arkansas summer night when tragedy struck in my front yard. I look forward to the day when I see my old friends, Royce and O'Neal, again. I am certain the ol' Cook boy will have those legs the next time I see him.

Not long after the O'Neal Cook tragedy that Emma and I were trying to erase from our minds, another highway misfortune happened within ten feet of the accident site. At about 8:30 p.m. one evening after Emma and I had just put our daughters to bed, there came another unexpected knock at our front door. I cautiously opened the door and found a well-dressed man standing on our porch.

The man quickly stepped back as if to communicate, "I mean no harm." He explained to me that he was driving a brand-new car and that he had a flat tire. He said that his spare had not been aired up—an obvious oversight by the dealership's mechanic who checked the car out at the time of the sale. The man told me that his wife and three little boys were in the disabled car across the road and that he and his family were on their way to Hot Springs. He asked to borrow our phone to call for help. I told the man he was welcome to use our phone, but I asked him to first tell me what kind of new car he had. He said, 'It's a Chevrolet Impala."

As luck would have it, I had just recently bought Emma a Chevrolet Impala. I said, "Sir, I have an idea that might just put you on the road again."

He mused, "Okay. What?"

"I will loan you my spare tire which will fit your car perfectly, and you can return it on your way back through." I thought I saw a tear in his eye as the man gave me a huge hug.

Because the man was not dressed to work on a car, I put my spare on his car and tossed the flat one into the trunk. As I worked, the man told me that he and his family lived in Longview, Texas, where he was manager of a Safeway grocery store. When the job of changing the tires was complete, the man thanked me excessively, then he drove away with his pretty wife and young children. Six days later, I went out early in the morning to get our newspaper. There on our front porch was my spare tire. For many years, Emma and I exchanged Christmas cards with our new Texas friends.

Although neither of the late-night Highway 7 incidents started out good, both left me with lasting friendships and gratitude that I was used as a vessel to help others. While I would never wish misfortune on anyone, it is a humbling life experience to be placed in positions that impacted the lives of others in meaningful ways.

To quote Hamlet: "There is nothing good or bad, but thinking makes it so."

Yet another roadside incident took place when I was traveling on Interstate 30 south of Little Rock in 1966. At that time, hood ornaments, also known as car mascots, were commonplace. Originally designed to camouflage unattractive radiator caps, hood ornaments became an ornamental aspect of automobile design and continued to be popular as hood accessories long after radiators were completely enclosed under the hoods of vehicles. The Rolls-Royce Spirit of Ecstasy and the Jaguar Leaper were among the most recognizable. Because I had a long road trip each day from my home to work and saw hundreds of vehicles each week, I thought I had seen every hood ornament known to man until one cold, January morning when I saw one like none I had ever seen before—or since, for that matter.

Howard Mayberry and I carpooled to work each day from our homes near Hot Springs, Arkansas, to Little Rock where we both worked. Howard was a long-time friend and fellow schoolteacher. We both lived well out in the country in opposite directions from the Spa City, so we rendezvoused at the corner of Central and Grand Monday through Friday and then made the one-hour commute to Little Rock where we both taught in the same junior high school building in the Little Rock Public School District. This ritual lasted for three and a half years.

Howard and I were both true country boys, living more like people of the 1850's than mid twentieth-century men. By necessity, we were early risers—typically rolling out of bed around 4:00 a.m. We started our days watering and feeding hogs, chickens, and cows. Then, we headed back inside to shave and get dressed for the classroom. Most of our food came from our farms. My precious Emma always had breakfast ready for me when I finished my morning chores. Before getting herself ready for the day, she prepared a meal that usually included ham or bacon, eggs, biscuits, and jelly. With a full stomach, I would then set out to meet up with my friend and co-worker for the long trek to the capitol city.

One cold and dreary winter day that started out like so many others took a most unexpected turn. Howard was driving and I was absorbed in a newspaper article in the *Arkansas Gazette* written by legendary sportswriter Orville Henry. As Howard and I tooled along Interstate 30, I was captivated by Henry's take on the Razorbacks when suddenly a car traveling in the same direction as we were on the service road to our right demanded our attention. An older model car driven by an attractive, well-dressed woman, was oddly transporting a disheveled and distressed man sprawled across the hood of the vehicle. The human hood ornament looked like he had been on an all-night drinking spree. He was wearing an unbuttoned shirt and was red-faced and barefoot.

As the woman sped down the road, the man clinging to the hood was screaming, "Help! Help! Help!"

Howard and I watched as driver after driver pulled up alongside the car and offered assistance only to be waved off by the pretty lady driver. I'm sure all the other travelers were just as mystified, confused, and amused as we were at the extraordinary sight. Howard laughed uncontrollably and his fat belly truly shook like a bowlful of jelly.

 We were going about seventy miles per hour parallel to the car on the service road. An onramp was just ahead. The woman would soon have to choose to either remain straight on the service road or merge left onto I-30. Low and behold, she chose to merge onto I-30 and seamlessly slid into the lane right beside us. I rolled my car window down and made motions offering to help. I recall that the female driver's countenance was as innocent and beautiful as images of Mother Mary cradling the Christ Child. The angelic-looking woman sweetly refused my offer and waved me off as she had done with everyone else who had offered aid. At that point, I suggested to Howard that he speed up and change lanes to avoid a collision with the pretty lady or her unconventional passenger whose situation became even more precarious when the car merged onto the interstate and increased speed. Howard took my advice. We quickly lost sight of the vehicle and resumed our familiar daily road trip.

With the fascinating experience behind us, I began to ponder the story that might have led up to that extraordinary situation. I speculated that the man (possibly the husband of the well-dressed woman) had a drinking problem and probably did not work. My theory was that the woman had gotten fixed up to drive to her job in Little Rock when her drunken husband came stumbling in after an all-night drinking spree.

My guess was that they were a one-car family and that they got into a fight over the car key. I supposed that the woman grabbed the car key, sprinted to the car, locked the doors, and proceeded to leave for work. I further presumed that the drunken husband, thinking he would prevent her from leaving, foolishly jumped onto the car hood. However, the woman had had enough of her husband's foolishness, so off to work she went with poor ol' Joe stretched across the slick hood of the car and hanging on for dear life. Unfortunately, I will never really know how that crazy escapade started or ended, but I had fun creating a story in my mind.

That's my speculation. Now it's your turn. What do you think?

The Hunting Cap Tunnel

If you have ever visited Hot Springs, Arkansas, chances are you may have missed its most unique landmark. Back in 1884, a one-mile-long tunnel was developed out of a Hot Springs creek bed. It begins in the rear of the First Presbyterian Church and meanders under Whittington Avenue, ending on Broadway Street. The story of that tunnel is fascinating, but it's not my story.

My story is about another tunnel in Hot Springs, Arkansas, only about sixty feet long. In 1957, I made my first visit to Oaklawn Racetrack and was "hooked." Going to horse races became my number one pastime for the next sixty years. I became quite good at my "second profession." That's not to say that I always came home a winner, but I did very well overall. Twice, I hit the lucrative "pick six" that has since been done away with.

Back in the 1980's on a pleasant, sunny day, I bumped into a long-time friend at the Oaklawn Racetrack. He often borrowed racing information from me; however, I was cautious, and you might even say "stingy," when it came to giving out my handicapping information. My friend asked about a favorite horse named Hunting Cap that would be running in the feature race. That horse was a strong favorite, bet down to 1-1. I remained noncommittal as my friend expressed his view that Hunting Cap would surely win the big race. I remembered something the great D. Wayne Lukas once told me about strong favorites.

He said, "But they gotta run the race." That stuck!

My friend then told me that he was betting five thousand dollars on Hunting Cap to win. He went to the fifty-dollar window and the clerk, Gene Axt, carefully counted my friend's five thousand dollars then handed him the tickets. Hunting Cap seemed like a sure bet, but I reminded my friend that those sure bets still have to run the race. My friend ignored my sage comment and walked to the porch fence to get a first-hand eye view of ol' Hunting Cap as he sped around the six-furlong oval.

To understand what happened, you need to know that Oaklawn management always catered to the racing fans. Fans were allowed to walk across the racing track between certain races to go to the infield. The heavy foot traffic left a trail of footprints in the soft dirt of the track.

It was time for the feature race of the day to begin. As soon as the gates opened and the race was on, Hunting Cap jumped to a quick lead. By the time he reached the Clubhouse turn, he had a clear five-length advantage over his closest rival. Hunting Cap's jockey never raised his whip.

Now, Hunting Cap was approaching the finish line, but oops! He discovered the trail of tracks created by fans crossing to the infield. Oops again! Like a trained equestrian horse, Hunting Cap leapt over the trail and lost enough ground in doing so to drop him back to second place. Now, he was one-half length behind his nearest competitor. Hunting Cap and his jockey tried furiously to regain the lead, but the other horse won by a head.

Guess what? The following spring when the gates opened for the first races of the season, there was a new tunnel dug under the track. It seemed hardly anyone other than me knew why my long-time friend who lost his five-thousand dollars the season before was never seen again at the Oaklawn Racetrack. To me, that tunnel will forever be known as "Hunting Cap Tunnel."

I barely knew Mr. John Cella, the head of Oaklawn. But as time marched on his son, Mr. Charles Cella, took over the reins as owner of the racetrack. I called him "Mr. High Pockets" because he wore his pants several inches above his ankles. There was an incident that caused us to become speaking friends until his death. Once while walking through Oaklawn's Jockey Club, Charles and I literally bumped into each other.

We exchanged the customary "Pardon me." I then said, "Hey, do you have a tip?" He smiled and said, "No."

After that, anytime we passed each other in the track, we would say, "Got a tip?"

Gambling Man

My passion for horse racing took Emma and me to some exciting events in beautiful locations including the Belmont Stakes near Elmont, New York, and Gulfstream Park Racing in Hallandale, Florida. Emma tolerated my gambling addiction. I, in turn, indulged her passion for the arts. We had some wonderful adventures as we traveled around the nation. I will share just a couple of the most memorable ones.

In 1973, Emma and I were on our second exciting round to watch the Belmont Stakes near Elmont, New York. We had learned from our first trip to wear our walking shoes. Our experience was worth every step because we had the privilege of watching the magnificent Secretariat. What an animal! As they say in Arkansas, "We thought we were something on a stick."

After a day filled with excitement and lots of walking, Emma and I were tuckered out and starving. Our problem was that we had no clue where to find a nice, sit-down restaurant. I spotted a friendly-looking gentleman walking toward us and stopped him. I asked if he could recommend a nice restaurant in the area.

He first started giving verbal directions, then quickly said, "I will show you." He walked us to the next corner then part of the way down an adjacent street where he suddenly stopped and said, "Up those stairs, but it's expensive."

I thanked him and shook his hand. Most of my adult life I had heard what terrible snobs New Yorkers were, but no one in our beloved South could have been more hospitable than the kind gentleman from the Big Apple who became our personal tour guide and accompanied us to a nice restaurant.

Emma and I were seated next to a well-dressed lady who was a little on the colorful side for the 1970's. We exchanged greetings.

After we ordered drinks, I said, "Excuse me ma'am, we are new to New York. Can you recommend something from the menu?" I had to ignore kicks on my shins under the table from you-know-who, but our next-table neighbor seemed pleased that I had asked.

"Yes, I can," she said with a nice smile then told me about two of her favorites. I thanked her, then she asked what part of the South we hailed from. She said, "Your beautiful wife gives it away, not you." That stopped the under-the-table kicking. Emma was aglow.

Then our new ~~fried~~ friend asked, "What is your occupation?"

I retorted that I was a plowboy. She looked puzzled, so I answered her unspoken question. "I get a plow between the mule and me, then I guide the animal as it tills the soil." She laughed so hard I am sure she must have wet her underwear.

She said, "Well, there's one thing I know about you. You don't always tell the truth." We were all laughing as she added, "You're a great storyteller."

We never circled back to the subject of my occupation, but Emma curiously asked our new acquaintance what hers was. Our flashy new acquaintance quickly responded, "I am the president of Chase Manhattan." She went on to talk about being a female in a high executive position. She seemed to enjoy telling us about herself and even shared stories about her earlier life. Eventually, she finished her meal and excused herself.

Now, do we really believe our dinner companion was the president of Chase Manhattan Bank? Maybe I'm a sucker, but I believe she was. Emma, on the other hand, believes that I was not the only one who fibbed about my occupation that evening.

A decade later, Emma and I had become veteran visitors to the Big Apple. During our 1983 trip, we stayed at the Waldorf Astoria. After another wonderful visit in New York, we were all packed up and ready to go home when an advertisement popped up on the television screen regarding an exhibit of the works of Pablo Picasso coming to the Metropolitan Museum of Art (MMoA) the following year. We didn't pay much attention to the television ad, but as we were checking out, the clerk handed us a brochure about the Picasso exhibit. When we returned to Arkansas and had time to read the pamphlet, we decided to add that to our itinerary for our next year's trip to New York.

When we returned to NYC the following year, the first order of business was to attend the Belmont Stakes. The next day was for Emma. I was happy to accompany her to the highly anticipated Picasso exhibit at the MMoA. Not knowing the two-hundred-dollar tickets to the exhibit sold out within days of the announcement, Emma and I got all ~~gussied~~ dressed up and headed into the city allowing plenty of time to purchase tickets before the doors opened. We went to several ticket venders who all informed us that there were no tickets available and that tickets had sold out months ago.

Emma was dressed to the hilt and looked absolutely stunning. She was a natural beauty who turned heads of men and women everywhere we went. I was so proud of her and became determined not to disappoint her.

The taxi driver who drove us to within walking distance of the MMoA said as we were getting out of his vehicle, "You have a long line ahead of you. You're going to have to wait a while." We traipsed our way toward the hundred-yard-long line of very well-dressed men and women. I approached one of the men and said, "Sir, are all these people in line to get tickets?"

He chuckled and said, "Gosh, no! Tickets have been sold out for almost a year. We are all just waiting for the doors to open."

During our visit to the Belmont Racetrack the day before, I had done very well. I had a large sum of money stashed in my best Sunday coat and was feeling a little cocky. I pulled out the thick stack of cash, showed it to Emma, and assured her I was going to get us in to see the exhibit one way or another. I could sense her displeasure with me for flashing my cash and for the half-baked scheme that she knew was formulating in my brain. I turned and took a quick survey of the stagnant line. My wheels turned frantically as I continued to develop my plan for acquiring tickets. When I turned back to speak to Emma, she had disappeared. I spotted her huddled behind a large metal electrical pole. We made eye contact, and I gave her an enthusiastic thumbs up. She quickly disappeared again.

What in the world was ol' John Buck going to do now? As I stood there gazing at the motionless line, my mind drifted back a few years and made a connection to experiences we had in Fayetteville, Arkansas, while waiting to watch the Razorback football team in action. "Woo-pig, sooie!" Ol' John Buck had inspiration that soon became a full-fledged plan. Time and time again, as we approached the Arkansas Razorback Stadium, we saw the same man standing facing the crowd of hog fans as they filed into the football arena. That fellow would lift his right hand skyward, holding up two fingers as he bellowed out the same twelve-word phrase at each and every game:

"I need two—one for me and one for you-know-who!" Interestingly, he always seemed to get his tickets—usually for free. Mimicking that cunningly brave soul's strategy, I made my way to the front of the very long line where I made a snappy about-face. I first took a long look at the large, shiny electrical pole concealing Emma. She was well hidden, but I could see two or three inches of her expensive black jacket moving with the breeze letting me know that she was still there.

I confidently thrust my hand high into the air with two fingers extended. I repeated the familiar refrain— "I need two—one for me and one for you-know-who." I began to slowly work my way down the line of all those elegant ticket holders, most of whom were New Yorkers. I smiled broadly and made eye contact with each one who would glance my way. My antics brought wide smiles and sometimes laughter as some of the folks in the line cheered me on with encouraging hoorays and emphatic yeses. I had only strode by fifteen or twenty people when an attractive older lady motioned me to her.

She said, "Young man, I have one extra ticket. If you can use just one, you may have it." I graciously accepted it and reached into my pocket to get money to pay her. She refused to accept my cash and seemed most pleased with her generous gift to a total stranger.

I only walked a few steps further when another, not so attractive, older lady motioned to me. She sheepishly said, "Sir, if there is any way you can use a ticket that is expired, I have one (for yesterday) that you may have." I enthusiastically accepted the worthless ticket. Again, I tried to pay the generous lady. She, too, refused to take my money.

I reunited with Emma, and we walked briskly to the end of the line with two free tickets to the sold-out exhibit. Now I had to conjure up another slick scheme to get past the ticket taker with that expired ticket. When the doors finally opened and the line began to snake toward the entrance of the museum, I carefully studied the ticket taker's habits and made mental notes of my observations which proved to be most helpful to this old plowboy from Arkansas. The middle-aged man colleting tickets was quite meticulous as he carefully examined each ticket. However, he had little tolerance for those who dawdled and allowed a gap to form and cause a momentary delay in the otherwise steady flow of the slow-moving line.

When someone broke the rhythm of the procession, the impatient ticket taker would hurriedly snatch the ticket from the hand of the person responsible for stalling progress while mumbling inaudible words that were probably best not heard. He would then toss the snatched ticket into a tall metal can without even looking at it. Wow! What a valuable observation!

With light bulbs popping off in my head, I solidified a plan to get us in to see the sold-out art exhibit. Maybe! I was as nervous as a long-tailed cat in a room full of rocking chairs as we approached the entrance door. I nudged Emma, who was holding the good ticket, and she moved forward a short distance. Then, to create a larger space between us, I put on an impressive coughing act. Mr. Uptight Ticker Taker was beside himself when the steady flow of the line came to an abrupt halt. As I continued coughing and hacking, I extended my arm so that yesterday's ticket was within his reach. True to form, he snatched that sucker from my hand and threw it perfectly into that tall metal can. Eureka! Drysdale himself never threw a more perfect strike.

Inside the museum, we meandered aimlessly from room to room looking at canvas after canvas with paint thrown on it. Of course, I am not a refined art lover, but it seemed to me one would need to be considerably "under the influence" to call splashes of paint on white canvases art. In my humble opinion, the most prized pieces of art are paintings of beautiful horses second only to those of gorgeous women. Third, are paintings of beautiful landscapes. Picasso's works could not compare to any of those. Now, argue with me! An old Arkansas saying came to this old country boy as I strolled through that grand building with my stunning wife: "You win some. You lose some. And some get rained out." Considering the price I did not pay for those coveted Picasso tickets, I realized it is true that you get what you pay for.

Some years later, I hopped a plane to Hallandale Beach, Florida, for a big race at Gulfstream Racetrack. I don't remember how I fared at the track that day, but an encounter I had the day after the races was one I have never forgotten. My habit was to always arrive early at the airport. The day after the races, I rose early, finished breakfast, and quickly brushed my teeth. I then called the front desk and requested that the front desk clerk call a taxi so that it would be waiting for me when I arrived in the lobby.

The hotel clerk took my name and said, "Your taxi will be here in twenty minutes." I grabbed my light luggage, made my way to the lobby, and went outside. As I approached the area marked Taxi, my ride was pulling in. I noticed a nice-looking gentleman, his equally attractive wife, and their young son rushing up behind me. They seemed to be running late and in a big hurry. They pressed their way past me and started loading their things into the taxi. The driver asked their name then informed them that he was there for Mr. Miller.

"That's me," I said.

The man immediately pulled back and apologized for his rudeness. He explained that their taxi had not yet arrived and that they were going to miss their flight. I said, "If it's okay with the driver, you can have my taxi."

The driver said, "Sure, if it's okay with you, Mr. Miller." With that, the little family quickly loaded into the taxi. I don't know if they made their flight or not, but I felt good about the part I played in helping them out—and that's not the end of this story.

Almost two years went by. A friend of mine who was almost always with me in those days, especially if I was going to the races, talked me into a day at Oaklawn Racetrack in Hot Springs, Arkansas. Actually, it didn't take much talking to persuade ol' John Buck to pay a visit to one of his favorite edifices. As the day dwindled down to the fifth or sixth race, my friend and I had gotten on the outside of a few Miller High Lifes, so it was time to visit the latrine.

All the urinals were taken, so my friend and I each chose a stall with a door. We were in adjacent stalls, so we struck up a conversation. We were talking loudly enough to hear each other and for others to hear, as well. My buddy finished up his business first and left his stall. The stranger waiting for the next stall did not immediately take the one left empty by my friend. He seemed more interested in our conversation than with the business at hand.

Speaking to my friend because I had not yet emerged, the stranger said, "I know who that voice belongs to."

Allen, my friend, asked, "Do we know you?"

The man replied, "I don't know you, but that man in there has a totally unique voice that I shall never forget. He befriended my family and me when we were in great need at a Holiday Inn in Hallandale Beach, Florida, about two years ago."

I came out of the stall eager to greet my old friend. I instinctively extended my arm for a handshake then awkwardly withdrew it, realizing that I had not yet washed my hands.

There was a brief, uncomfortable moment, then my friend of two years said, "What the heck," and gave me a robust hug. It was a joyful reunion, but too brief for all of us. I do not recall how I fared with the ponies at Oaklawn that day, but it's always a winning day when great memories are made with friends—old and new.

Tom and Jerry

In 1995, our younger daughter, Michelle and her husband moved from their home in Little Rock, Arkansas, to a very nice neighborhood in Austin, Texas. It was an upscale neighborhood where all the women wore silk panties rather than cotton drawers. Our daughter's huge, high-dollar home had a large pool in the back yard and a mother-in-law's quarters upstairs where Emma and I were frequent guests. The rows of houses were built back-to-back with tall, wooden privacy fences separating the sixty-five-foot-deep back yards and obstructing the views of neighbors. It is Michelle's fence that is a significant part of this story.

The fence in my daughter's back yard was at the far end of her pool, about four feet beyond it. The old fence had deteriorated and was separated in one spot leaving a gap large enough for a person to squeeze through. And slither through that narrow opening is exactly what Michelles' backdoor neighbor, Tom, did. Once he made his way through, I was there to greet him on our side.

Tom was an intriguing man. Except for that first act of boldness that brought us face to face, everything else about his demeanor suggested that he was an introvert. His shy personality was puzzling to me. Even after getting to know him, I still wondered where he got the courage to slide through that breach in the privacy fence to visit with me in Michelle's backyard—something that became an almost daily routine. From our first encounter, Tom engaged with me as if we had known each other all our lives.

Not long after our friendship started, Tom decided to replace the rickety fence. Much to our surprise, Tom had his contractors install a two-way gate in the new structure to allow for easy passage from his yard to Michelle's and vice versa. Tom did not ask our consent, so we wondered if the gate was legal. We decided not to say anything to ol' Tom about it. It was obvious to us that he was lonesome and needed ol' John Buck's friendship.

I once shared with Tom that the Miller family had a loose connection with Texas legend and owner of the Dallas Cowboys, Jerry Jones. During the time the Jones family lived in Little Rock, Arkansas, their home was right around the corner from ours. Their daughter, Charlotte, and Michelle were classmates at the historic Little Rock Central High School.

Years before being neighbors with the Jerry Jones family, I was associated in a young insurance company with Jerry's father and uncle, Pat and Paul. The brothers had previously owned a grocery store in North Little Rock that burned to the ground. According to James H.

Hall, a partner of ours and a friend of mine, the insurance payout for the grocery store was twenty thousand dollars—a considerable sum of money back in the 1950's. Fortunately for the Jones brothers, at the time of their payout, there were several insurance charters lying dormant around the State that could be purchased for a song. Pat and Paul purchased and activated a charter and became very rich from their twenty-thousand-dollar investment. They soon sold their stock in Arkansas and headed to Missouri to repeat their efforts, only bigger.

Pat's son, Jerry, became a linebacker at the University of Arkansas playing for the great Frank Browles. After graduating from the U of A, Jerry, having access to the family fortune, began speculating in gas and oil in western Arkansas along the Oklahoma border. He hit it rich. Soon the Dallas Cowboys came up for sale, and the rest is history. My friend on the other side of the fence never said so, but I sensed he did not fully believe all that I told him about my Jerry Jones connection, as weak as the connection was. Then one afternoon when Tom and I were engaged in our daily ritual of chatting beside the pool, Emma called to me from the backdoor and told me I had a telephone call. I asked, "Who is it?"

Emma replied, "It's Jerry Jones."

"Tell him I'm busy. I'll call him back later."

Something I had never told Tom was that I had another friend whose name also just happened to be Jerry Jones. Dr. Jerry Jones and his lovely wife, Susan, once bought a house from Emma and me. They became our dear friends and fellow church members. Without that tidbit of information about "the other Jerry Jones," ol' through-the-fence Tom assumed the caller was Dallas Cowboys' owner Jerry Jones. His face skipped red and turned pasty white. He was struck speechless as he incorrectly assumed that I had delayed talking to Jerry Jones—money mogul and owner of arguably the greatest sports team in the United States—in favor of completing our backyard chat. Tom lingered only briefly without saying another word then silently slipped back through the newly installed gate and slowly trudged home. I didn't see Tom for three days. When our daily visits resumed, the subject of Jerry Jones never came up again.

The Last Chapter

Life. Since the beginning of time, poets, songwriters, and philosophers have mused life's meaning. In their attempts to convey a simple definition, they have created countless analogies of the concept of life. Yet, the question lingers: "What is life?"

This is my assessment. If life is a tapestry, mine is among the most colorful. If life is a race, I believe I have run it well thus far and still have plenty of stamina left to make a few more laps before entering the home stretch. If life is a lump of clay being cast and recast on a potter's wheel in pursuit of an acceptable vessel, then I am still a work in progress. If life is truly a box of chocolates, mine is an assortment of sweet ones, bitter ones, bittersweet ones, nutty ones, and a whole slew of mystery-filled ones.

One of my life's most unexpected encounters happened for me when, at the age of thirteen, I was returning home from church and was about halfway there. I was in a bit of a hurry because I was hungry and eagerly anticipating what Mom might have cooked up for dinner. As I walked past my aunt and uncle's pond, I saw them along with their three-year-old daughter, Darlene, enjoying a beautiful Sunday afternoon. I decided to stop long enough to say hello. As I approached, little Darlene was splashing in the edge of the pond on the bank nearest to me. My aunt and uncle were on the far side of the pond. As I drew closer, the little girl abruptly stood up and took off toward the center of the pond. She suddenly slipped into water that was over ten feet deep. It was obvious to me that the child was in over her head, literally, and that she could not swim. Her parents were too far away to get to her in time to save her. Despite being decked out in my "Sunday best," I instinctively dove into the pond, quickly located and took hold of little Darlene, and swam to the surface while keeping a firm grasp on the child. Her parents were overjoyed that I saved my little cousin's life. I was, too, and forgot all about being hungry.

As a kid, I could never have dreamed of how blessed I would be in life. Growing up in that little two-room shanty with cracks in the shingle roof and gaps in the log walls, I was unaware that such things as electric lights, air conditioners, gas furnaces, indoor plumbing, toothbrushes, and toilet paper on a cardboard roll existed. My children and grandchildren have not had lives without challenges and struggles, but I am thankful they have never experienced abject poverty in the way I did.

One thing that was especially important to me when I became a father was for my children to never know the feeling of going to bed hungry and waking up to find little or no groceries in the house. Perhaps due to the lack of food in our home when I was growing up, food became the cornerstone of celebrations big and small for our little family. As soon as Emma and I got our bachelor's degrees and began our careers in education, it became our monthly practice (because teachers only got paid once a month) to drive to Hot Springs to buy groceries.

When we got home, we treated ourselves to cheeseburgers, fried potatoes, iced tea, and cobbler with ice cream. We took to our new ability to splurge once a month like ducks to water. Emma's parents lived with us for a few years and joined right in on our new monthly family tradition. Years later when we moved to Little Rock in 1968, we improved on the ritual. We adjusted the schedule to a weekly event and substituted tater tots for fried potatoes. In addition, we added a Friday evening treat of going to Franke's or Wyatt's, two of our favorite cafeteria-style restaurants, and then on to Baskin Robbins for ice cream. We thought we were living high on the hog.

In the early months of our marriage, my beautiful, curvy bride could not boil water without burning it, but she soon became an excellent cook. Our Sunday lunch was almost always roast beef with all the trimmings including potatoes, carrots, greens, and rolls along with homemade pie for dessert. While we lived in the country, we had a vegetable garden where we grew tomatoes, squash, okra, beans, onions, corn, and beets. We also raised our own hogs, calves, and chickens. Once a week, Emma would fry up three chickens. Her homemade fried chicken put Colonel Sander's to shame. To complement her Southern entrée, she usually cooked up mashed potatoes, white gravy, sliced bread, green beans, and dessert. We ate it all with very little left over.

I taught both of our daughters how to lie and steal on chicken-frying days. Both girls were excellent students. In fact, they were naturals. Either of them could snatch a chicken leg and destroy the evidence in a flash and then take their seats at the kitchen table as if they were famished. They made their Daddy proud.

After our move to Little Rock, we sometimes made the drive to beautiful Hot Springs, Arkansas, just to get away from the city for a while. We often stopped at a little family-owned restaurant called Taco Shack. I would buy a big bag of tacos to take home with us. On the way back to Little Rock, Emma and our older daughter, Leticia, might eat one or two tacos before passing the bag to our younger daughter, Michelle, in the back seat. That tiny salivating piranha in the rear of the car could polish off a bag of tacos faster that you could say Jack Robinson. Emma and I decided that Michelle's pretty little legs must be hollow. It didn't matter how many tacos I bought; the bag was always empty when we got home, leaving none for me. I never minded. It gave me more joy to know how much little Michelle enjoyed my food purchase than a few tacos would have given me.

From 1959 until 1967 Art Linkletter hosted a radio and television program with a feature segment called "Kids Say the Darndest Things." Although my children and grandchildren were never featured on television, they sure said and did some things that cracked me up. I'll share a few from each of my descendants.

Leticia.

• When she was two or three years old, I caught her reaching into the flour tin with both hands and then dropping the fistfuls of flour onto her head. She had obviously been doing that for quite some time before I discovered her because when I walked in on her, she looked like Casper the Friendly Ghost. All I could do was scoop her up and give her a big hug. She said, "Daddy, I just had to."

• While still a toddler and trying to outrun her Daddy, Leticia said, "Faster, legs, faster."

• At about four years old, Leticia recited lines she had learned in Sunday School to our very large church congregation. She was absolutely adorable as she belted out, "My speech is short, but friends it's true. I'm BERRY glad to welcome you."

Michelle.

- When she was a wee one, anytime we were in the car and she saw heavy machinery, she would say, "Dad, it's dain-gee-us. Ess get outta hee-uh."

- When Michelle was eight and we were taking a road trip from Little Rock to Dallas to go to Six Flags, she announced that she was going to set a world record for *not* napping while riding in the back seat. Unless the world record was less than five minutes, she did not succeed.

- Interestingly, Michelle could not learn colors. When she was ten years old, I pointed to a large yellow road sign and said, "I don't know what color that is." Michelle responded, "I don't know either, Dad."

Layne.

- Our first grandson always woke at the butt crack of dawn when he spent the night with us. Jugi and I were always awakened to Layne loudly chanting, "Sun's up. Sun's up. Sun's up."

- Layne was also keen at spotting "cherry pickers." He never missed one and would always say, "Look, Jugi, there's a cherry picker."

- When he was about four, Layne tagged along with me when I went to work on a neighbor's lawn mower. Our neighbor, Mr. Shelton, was fumbling for words. Layne said, "Mr. Shelton could it be that your brain is confused?"

Neal.

- Neal was not a fan of baseball when he was little. On our way home from an Arkansas Traveler's game he said, "The next time we go to a ballgame, I'm gonna stay home."

- When he was about four, Neal was riding in the car with his Aunt Michelle. He had fallen asleep and was suddenly awakened. Startled, he sat up and said, "Where in the h--- are we?"

Grace.

- Our first granddaughter was competitive even at the age of five. When playing a softball game with Jugi and me, Grace became very frustrated with her grandfather and said, "Papaw, don't you know the rules?"

- At the age of six, Grace was unable to say the word quiet. Instead, she said, "fi-et." I corrected her and said, "No, sweetheart. It's quiet." She retorted, "That's what I said. Be fi-et."

- When Grace was about seven, I put her up to asking her teacher what the first thing is that a little boy takes hold of when he goes outside to pee. I equipped her with the answer: the doorknob. I thought it was a funny joke. However, when Grace posed the question at school, her poor teacher was in total shock and exclaimed, "Where did you hear that?" Her reply: "From Papaw." I guess the real joke was on me.

Hope. Last but not least, came our fiery-spirited baby of the family.

- When Hope was three, Jugi was bragging about how pretty Hope looked and said, "You look like a little princess." Hope responded, "I not a princess. I da queen!"
- Once when I had corrected Hope for something, she snapped, "Papaw, don't say those words to me."
- Another time, Hope's father was spraying weed poison on the lawn and told Hope to get off the grass. She fired back, "YOU get off the grass."

Family. They say there's not a single one without some degree of dysfunction. Mine is no exception. However, my deepest love and greatest joys are derived from Emma and those who share our DNA. I am so thankful God assigned them to me.

Both Emma and I had long careers in education. Emma taught school for thirty-three years. I taught for nine and a half years then went to work for the Arkansas Department of Education for the next twenty-three years. During the years that I was a teacher, I taught Bill Clinton and best-selling American author E. Lynn Harris. As most teachers can attest, I learned more during my tenure than any of my students. In fact, I am convinced that we are all students from birth to the grave. I have learned so many life truths along the way on this journey of life.

From my early years, I learned that what doesn't kill us truly makes us stronger and that life's most valuable treasures cannot be purchased with money. From my little cousin, Darlene, I learned that saving a life is a cure for hunger. From my military years, I learned that family by love is sometimes more precious than family by blood. From my wife, I learned my own worth as well as the futility of trying to win the affection of someone who does not know his own worth. From O'Neal Cook, I learned that no matter what life throws your way, keeping a positive attitude is the key to success and survival. From my children and grandchildren, I've learned that the breadth of a father's/grandfather's love is limitless.

What lies ahead for ol' John Buck remains a mystery. One thing I know for sure is that life is unpredictable. Benjamin Franklin once said that "in this world nothing is certain except death and taxes." With that premise in mind, one of the secrets to happiness and contentment in life is to embrace the present. With almost nine decades in the review mirror, I vow to live every day that God gives me. I will never be one to merely exist. As long as my body and mind remain strong, I intend to continue this journey with gusto, making new friends and collecting more precious memories along the way. My beloved readers, if I don't have the joy of meeting you this side of Glory, be assured that I will catch you on the flip side.

So long 'til we gather in the nest of that Great Speckled Bird above.

THE END